"In *How to Understand the Bible*, one of the best contemporary Mennonite Bible expositors shows us how to mine the treasures of the sacred text faithfully and relevantly. The book is marked by great respect for Scripture, balanced judgments on the tough issues, and a readable style. Abundant illustrations of every aspect of interpretation make the material highly understandable and useful even to the nonexpert."
—*George R. Brunk III, Professor of New Testament, Eastern Mennonite Seminary, Harrisonburg, Virginia*

"David Ewert demonstrates superb understanding of issues pertinent to reading and interpreting the Bible. With plain speech and a direct style, Ewert harnesses the insights of critical scholarship in an effort to improve biblical literacy among the body of believers. Cultural, textual, and hermeneutic issues are introduced and explained, with appropriate examples provided for illustrative purposes. The result is a quite usable guide for serious students of the Scriptures."
—*Jay Wade Marshall, Presidential Dean, Earlham School of Religion, Richmond, Indiana*

"Interpretation is more than a literary science; at the deepest level, it depends on the spirit of the interpreter. As Ewert makes clear in his introduction, none of us comes to the Bible without presuppositions; each of us has a perspective.

"The author calls us honestly to read the Scripture for what it said in the time, culture, and language of the writer, and then carefully interpret its intent in the context of our time and culture.

"The book will be helpful to all evangelical readers as it spans denominational lines. Standing in the continuum of Anabaptist theology, I looked for evidence that the author related the Testaments as promise to fulfillment, that he emphasized the will of God as modeled in the life of Jesus, and that he focused on the relation of Spirit and letter.

"I especially affirm Ewert's emphasis on the Holy Spirit's work in helping us understand the Scriptures. Readers will also have particular interests arising from their own theological orientation; on these we need to be honest and open to the Spirit and the Word.

"This book can be of particular benefit for the thousands of small groups that meet for Bible study, as well as for careful work in the Christian education programs in congregations across the spectrum of Christian faith. The Scripture is our authority as God's self-disclosure culminating in Christ; therefore, we must be sure that we hear Christ as we read his Word."

—*Myron S. Augsburger, Evangelist; Adjunct Professor of Theology, Eastern Mennonite Seminary; former President of Coalition of Christian Colleges and Universities*

How to Understand the Bible

David Ewert

Herald
Press

Waterloo, Ontario
Scottdale, Pennsylvania

Canadian Cataloguing-in-Publication Data
Ewert, David, 1922-
How to understand the Bible
Includes bibliographical references.
ISBN 0-8361-9115-3
1. Bible—Hermeneutics. 2. Bible—Criticism, interpretation, etc.
   I. Title
BS476.E88 2000   220.6   C00-930408-8

The paper used in this publication is recycled and meets the minimum
requirements of American National Standard for Information Sciences—
Permanence of Paper for Printed Library Materials, ANSI Z39.48-1984.

Except as otherwise noted, the Bible text is from the *New Revised Standard
Version Bible*, copyright © 1989 by the Division of Christian Education of the
National Council of the Churches of Christ in the USA, and is used by per-
mission. There are brief comparisons to GNB, *Good News Bible*; KJV, *King
James Version, The Holy Bible*; NEB, *New English Bible*; RSV, *Revised Standard
Version Bible*; CEV, *Contemporary English Version*.

HOW TO UNDERSTAND THE BIBLE
Copyright © 2000 by Herald Press, Waterloo, Ont. N2L 6H7.
   Published simultaneously in USA by
   Herald Press, Scottdale, Pa. 15683. All rights reserved
Canadiana Entry Number: C00-930408-8
Library of Congress Catalog Card Number: 00-190100
International Standard Book Number: 0-8361-9115-3
Printed in the United States of America

09 08 07 06 05 04 03 02 01 00 10 9 8 7 6 5 4 3 2 1

To order or request information,
please call 1-800-759-4447 (individuals); 1-800-245-7894 (trade).
Website: www.mph.org

To the late Dr. Abram H. Unruh,
whose careful exposition of the Scriptures
inspired me in my youth

Contents

Foreword

For many centuries past and likely many to come, biblical interpretation more than any other issue has aggravated the unity and shalom of the church. As we begin the twenty-first century, the problem is intensified on one hand by increasing biblical illiteracy, and on the other by increasing ideological polarization.

Books abound on hermeneutical strategies for scholars. But not many have appeared recently that have sought to connect with lay leadership in the church, written at the semipopular level. Therefore, Ewert's contribution in this volume is especially welcomed.

Ewert makes it possible for lay leadership, and scholars as well, to interact with basic issues in biblical interpretation. These issues range from the Bible's use of symbolism and its importance for interpretation, to the relationship between the Testaments. In two separate chapters, he also includes a quite thorough and helpful presentation of various literary genres used in the Old and New Testaments. One chapter focuses on the use of the Old Testament in and by the New.

The strength of Ewert's writing is its clarity, use of numerous cases to illustrate his points, and choice quotes to make the points stick. To illustrate the latter, in his discussion of word studies (philology), he quotes Nathan Söderblom of Sweden: "Philology is the eye of the needle though which the theological camel enters the kingdom of heaven" (61). Many other choice quotes and illustrations lace the pages of his book.

Actually, this volume is more than a handbook on

biblical interpretation. It includes a short history of the origins and translations of the biblical text. There is a wealth of specific textual illustrations, such as on the variety of biblical genres, with illustrative content. Hence, the book contains elements of basic biblical introduction, providing much information about the text and the culture behind the text. Thus one learns much about the Bible's content as well as about interpretation.

In this comprehensive overview of aspects of biblical interpretation, Ewert frequently tackles some of the hard issues encountered while explaining the Bible. One example is how to understand the apparent contradiction between 1 Corinthians 11:1-14 and 14:34-35 on the role of women in worship. He summarizes ten different interpretive proposals and indicates which of these are plausible and which impossible when considered against the overall guidelines and principles of biblical interpretation (121-4).

Suitable for study in the congregation, this resource has the potential to move the church on to firmer ground, decreasing biblical illiteracy and ideological polarization. I commend it as a book that both informs and blesses.

—*Willard M. Swartley*
Professor of New Testament
Associated Mennonite Biblical Seminary
Elkhart, Indiana

Preface

*E*vangelical Christians around the world confess that the Scriptures are their ultimate authority in matters of faith and practice. Yet such a mental and verbal confession does not always translate into lives that are shaped by the Word of God. But where else shall believers go for dependable guidance in doctrinal and ethical issues?

The *Confession of Faith in a Mennonite Perspective* in its article on "Scripture" puts it pointedly: "Other claims on our understanding of Christian faith and life, such as tradition, culture, experience, reason, and political powers, need to be tested and corrected by the light of Holy Scripture" (21-22; see Bibliography).

Human reason is too limited; it cannot answer the deepest questions of our existence—concerning guilt, suffering, or death. Human experience is not a trustworthy guide either, for it is diverse, and we are left with too many options. Conscience is not an infallible guide; it functions in keeping with what we think is right. It also can be sluggish, overly sensitive, or deformed. People who acted in good faith have committed some of the worst atrocities in history.

The Holy Spirit is our one sure guide as we seek to live the Christian life. However, the Spirit of God guides his people through the Word of God as found in the Scriptures in the context of the believing community. We are right to claim that Jesus Christ is our ultimate authority in matters of faith and ethics. But we need to remember that what we know about Jesus and his teachings also comes to us from the Holy Scriptures.

In the end, we must confess with the sixteenth-century Reformers, both mainline and Anabaptist, that the Bible alone is our ultimate authority and guide in a world that is often confusing.

Since we agree that we want to live according to the teachings of the Bible, we must ask, What does the Bible teach? Bible readers often have profound disagreements over what the Scriptures actually say. Moreover, the biblical writers do not speak directly to many issues believers face today. Hence, readers of the Bible do not always come to the same conclusions as they try to apply the teachings of the Scriptures to modern life.

I have written the following chapters with the hope that they might help us understand and apply the Word of God to our lives.

The reader may ask, Why another book on interpreting the Bible? It's a valid question. Serious readers of the Bible have access to many books on this topic. Some of them are more technical and do not appeal to the general student of the Scriptures. Others are somewhat limited in scope. Still others focus on the history of biblical interpretation.

In this volume, I try to use nontechnical language in dealing with a large range of topics of biblical interpretation. For the most part, it will leave the history of interpretation aside. Although I write as a member of a body of believers that has its roots in the Anabaptist movement of the sixteenth century, readers from other religious traditions may find this book helpful.

I have learned much from other writers on this subject and cannot claim originality in my treatment of the various topics discussed. Nevertheless, in the arrangement or the development of these topics, I have not followed any particular authority in biblical *hermeneutics* (a study of methods of interpreting). Some of the illustrations have become so much a part of my thinking that I cannot trace their source. I have not used footnotes, but I have added a list of texts in the bibliography. These sources may help those who would like to pursue the study of hermeneutics further.

Reading books on biblical interpretation is like learning the rules of a game. We can memorize the rules of the game, but that does not yet mean that we can play the game. We learn the rules of the game by playing. Whether I have "played the game" of interpreting the Bible well in my life, I will let others judge. In this area of study, we always remain learners.

I trust, however, that I may help others by sharing some of the things I have learned through many years of living with the Bible. My prayer is that this modest handbook of interpretation will lead many to a better understanding of the Word of God.

—David Ewert
  Professor Emeritus of Biblical Studies
  Canadian Mennonite University, Winnipeg

1

The Meaning and Significance of Hermeneutics

With unsearchable wisdom and grace, God chose to make himself known to the human race. Prophetically gifted individuals, who were divinely called, gave ancient Israel messages from God. When the time was fulfilled, God spoke to humankind by his Son, Jesus Christ (Heb. 1:1-2). The apostles bore witness to this final revelation in Christ.

Among the prophets and apostles were those who were led to record or dictate their inspired insights into God's plan of salvation. *Hermeneutics* deals with the interpretation of these ancient documents in the Bible.

Those prophets of Israel who recorded their messages (we do not have writings from some prophets) did so in Hebrew and the related Aramaic language. The apostles wrote in Greek. Writing materials were available to the biblical writers from the days of Moses. Because the manuscripts they produced were subject to wear and tear, many scribes throughout the centuries labored diligently to produce accurate new copies.

The copyists were eager to transcribe the original documents. Translators also assumed the painstaking task of turning these writings into other languages for readers who did not know Hebrew or Greek.

Today there is hardly a major people group that does not have the Bible in its native tongue. With the increase of literacy, people all over the world can now read the Scriptures for themselves. But the ability to read does not guarantee that Bible readers will always understand the teachings of the Bible in the same way. Thus the question, "Do you understand what you are reading?" is quite in place.

This is what the evangelist Philip asks the Ethiopian, who has gone to Jerusalem to worship (Acts 8:26-40). The Ethiopian is reading the prophet Isaiah while going home by chariot. In the custom of the time, he reads aloud. (We read, for example, of Cicero, who apologized to a friend for waiting so long to read the letter he had received from him, because he had a sore throat.)

Guided by the Spirit of God, Philip approaches the chariot and listens as this traveler reads Isaiah 53. To witness to him about Jesus, Philip engages the Ethiopian in conversation: "Do you understand what you are reading?"

He must have asked this question in a respectful tone, for such a question easily could have offended the traveler. Imagine that you are reading a book or newspaper and a stranger asks whether you understand what you are reading! But the Ethiopian is not offended; he invites Philip to sit in the chariot beside him and open the meaning of the prophetic passage he is reading. That is what hermeneutics is all about, finding the meaning of the Scriptures.

The Meaning of Hermeneutics

Reading a piece of literature is more complicated than engaging in a conversation. In conversation, we can hear the tone of the speakers and see their facial expressions and other bodily gestures. But when we read a book, we have only the written page before us. When the book we are reading happens to be thousands of years old, we have every reason to ask with the evangelist Philip, "Do you understand what you are reading?"

The interpretation of a document is called "hermeneutics." The Greek verb *hermeneuō* means to interpret, to translate, and to explain. The noun *hermeneia* signifies the practice of interpretation. The person who does the interpreting is called a *hermeneutēs*. Hence, *hē hermeneutikē technē* is the art or skill of interpretation, translation, or explication.

In Greek mythology, Hermes was the herald or messenger of Zeus. Hence, the word *hermeneutics*, coming from the name *Hermes*, is not a theological word. It is used generally for the interpretation of any piece of literature. However, the word family does appear in the Bible.

In the Septuagint (the Greek translation of the Old Testament), it is not found very often, but it is used. For example, Joseph at first spoke to his brothers through a *hermeneutēs*, "a translator" (Gen. 42:23). It is more common in the New Testament (NT). Jesus, for example "interpreted" the Scriptures for the Emmaus disciples (Luke 24:27, with the compound *diermeneuō*). One of the gifts of the Spirit is *hermeneia*, "interpretation" (1 Cor. 12:10; 14:26).

The word is also used for translation from one language to another. In John 1:38 we read: "Rabbi (which translated means Teacher), where are you staying?" In John 1:41, Andrew says to his brother, Simon, "We have found the Messiah (which is translated Anointed)." The compound *methermeneuō* appears in both of these passages.

Hermeneutics, then, has to do with the practice, the

skill, the art, the gift, and the science of interpretation. Since our concern is to interpret the Bible, we can appropriately speak of "biblical" hermeneutics. Bible readers may not know the word *hermeneutics* and may not be acquainted with the long history of biblical hermeneutics. Nevertheless, they are certainly interpreters (*hermeneutai*). Anyone who reads a passage from the Bible and asks what it might mean is practicing hermeneutics.

Basically, we must ask ourselves two questions when we read the Bible:

- What did these words mean for the ancient writers and readers?
- How do we apply this ancient text to our situation today?

It is important for Bible readers to keep a balance between these two questions.

Some biblical scholars are interested primarily in the original meaning of a text—vocabulary, grammar, literary forms, context, and so forth. That is where biblical interpretation must begin. But we have done only half our job if we simply immerse ourselves in the ancient world. If God's Word is to be kept alive and relevant, we must bring it across many centuries into our own everyday life.

There is also the opposite danger. Believers may become so caught up in what has been called the "relevance complex," that they hardly bother to ask what the text originally meant. As we interpret the Bible, we must try to maintain a healthy balance and interaction between these two concerns.

We might think that after several thousand years of Bible reading, most of the hermeneutical questions would have been answered. That sadly is not the case. Furthermore, our definition of hermeneutics includes the *application* of the biblical message to life today.

Hence, every generation of believers must hear once again what the Spirit of God is saying to them through these ancient texts.

Nevertheless, we can learn much from the history of biblical interpretation. Because most of the standard works on hermeneutics have a (shorter or longer) section on the history of interpretation, we dispense with such a survey in this book. Yet now and then, we do refer to the way Scriptures were understood in the past.

In spite of a long history of interpretation, the quarrels among Bible readers over what the Scriptures are actually saying to us are perhaps more acute today than ever before. On one of my teaching stints in the Ukraine, I discovered that an evangelical church had discontinued its midweek Bible studies. They did this because their debates over the meaning of the biblical text led to acrimony and dissension among the members of the church.

There is hardly a biblical topic that is not hotly debated in or between churches somewhere in this world today. Whether it's the teaching of the Bible about God, Jesus Christ, the Holy Spirit, salvation, the church, or eschatology—all of these topics are understood somewhat differently by believers in local churches all over the world.

This shouldn't surprise us. After all, two people can read the same article in a newspaper or magazine and understand it differently. There is an added complication in the case of the Scriptures; they were originally written in languages other than English, for people living in circumstances quite different from ours. We therefore expect that the biblical text will not always be understood in the same way by every Bible reader. There is, then, every good reason for publishing one more handbook in the area of hermeneutics.

The Significance of Hermeneutics

People of the same culture, living in the same period of history, speaking the same language, do not find it overly difficult to communicate in writing. Writers assume that readers are familiar with the subject under discussion. The situation, however, is much more complex when literature produced in a different culture, in times past, and written in a different language, is to be understood in more or less the same way by modern readers.

This situation would not be so critical if we were seeking to understand a piece of writing from a secular poet, historian, or fiction writer. In those cases, our lives do not depend on the correct interpretation of such literature.

The matter is much more serious, however, when we try to understand the message of the Bible. We believe that the Bible is God's word to humankind. Our understanding of the Bible and our response to it will determine how we live here on earth *and* will have profound implications for our eternal destiny. So we should be happy for any help we can receive in gaining a better understanding of the Holy Scriptures.

Not all Bible readers feel the need for guidance in the study of the Scriptures. They claim that the Scriptures are already sufficiently clear. They insist that we need only to read God's Word and obey it.

We reply that not all passages of Scripture are immediately plain. Nor do equally devout believers always agree on what the biblical authors are saying. Nevertheless, the Bible certainly is accessible to all who are interested in its message and the good news of salvation.

A seminary professor tells of a student who burst into tears during a seminar on principles of interpreting the Bible. The professor, afraid he said something that offended the student, asked, "What's wrong?"

"I'm crying because I feel sorry for you."

"Why do you feel sorry for me?"

"Because it is so hard for you to understand the Bible. I just read it, and God shows me the meaning" (from Klein: 4; see Bibliography).

This can be a dangerous and individualistic approach. If true, it means that God says different things to different people from the same texts of Scripture. However, we all need some guidance if we are to avoid interpreting the Scriptures in a completely subjective or arbitrary manner. We need to use good methods and to test our insights with fellow believers, to whom God's Spirit is also speaking (1 Cor. 14:26-29; 1 Thess. 5:21).

What makes understanding the Bible more difficult than grasping a story, a poem, or a treatise written in current English, using vocabulary common to those with a modest level of reading ability?

First, we are far removed from the Bible in terms of *time.* The books of the NT are almost two thousand years old, not to mention the much older Old Testament (OT) books. The prophets and apostles who have given us these literary documents spoke to their generation. Therefore, we must not read our worldview back into the biblical texts.

We certainly are not permitted to impose modern scientific insights on the biblical writers. It is not always easy for Bible readers, living in a sophisticated technological society, to hear what the prophets, Jesus, or the apostles were saying long ago to people living in circumstances so different from ours.

Since the books of the Bible were written, the world has changed so much that we are often at a loss to know what the biblical writers are talking about. Some of these writers were eyewitnesses to great historical events of which we know little. We look to ancient historians and archaeologists to help us understand what these ancient writers were talking about.

Second, we are not only far removed from the original writers and readers in time, but also in *culture*. Even though many people in Bible times lived in cities, societies in those days were mostly agrarian. Agricultural tools were primitive and bear little resemblance to our high-tech machinery. Travel was slow and wearisome, done mostly on foot. People wore clothing different from what we wear today.

The customs of ancient Israel, or those of the Greeks and the Romans, are in many respects foreign to us. What, for example, does it mean when Boaz takes off his sandal to confirm a transaction (Ruth 4:7-8)? Why would Barnabas lay the money he realized from the sale of real estate at the apostles' feet (Acts 4:37)?

We must be careful, then, not to interpret the Bible in the light of customs of our society. A knowledge of the marriage customs, economic practices, legal systems, methods of warfare, and the like, in the ancient Near East will greatly help us in interpreting the Bible.

Third, to understand the Bible, we must have some knowledge of the *geography* of the ancient world. We need to know something about the rivers of the Mediterranean world—the Tigris and Euphrates, the Nile and the Jordan, the Orontes and the Tiber. Mountains play a significant role in the history of Israel, as well as in the life and ministry of Jesus our Lord. We need to know the location of these mountains, as well as the plains, not to mention the many cities that are mentioned in the Bible.

We would find it hard to understand the Gospels unless we knew where the Sea of Galilee was situated. Even expressions such as "going up to Jerusalem" and "going down to Jericho" can be understood only if we know something about the geography of Palestine.

Fourth, there is a huge *language* gap between the books of the Bible and modern English. Biblical hermeneutics has the task of formulating rules for bridging this gulf between the Hebrew, Aramaic, and Greek languages of the Scriptures and our mother tongue. The many English versions available today bear witness to the fact that translating these ancient biblical texts into a modern tongue is not easy.

Translation is not simply matching English words with those in the Hebrew and Greek Testaments; that is next to impossible because of the lack of exact equivalents. Instead, we must try, insofar as possible, to capture the significance of what the original writer wanted to convey in sentences and paragraphs. Then we have to recast the message in a modern idiom.

Most Bible readers use translations when they search the Scriptures. Hence, they depend on others who have the linguistic equipment to put the meaning of the original texts into current English. Languages have been called "the speaking face of the heart." They represent much more than a different vocabulary or sentence structures; they are a reflection of the cultures of the people speaking them.

This means that unless we understand the *idioms* found in the languages of these ancient texts, we will not truly capture the messages of the biblical writers. The following chapters present more on all these matters.

Nevertheless, the gap between our world and the world of the Bible is bridgeable. Although humankind today is in so many ways far removed from the worlds of the Bible, there are many factors that remain constant in human history.

By familiarizing ourselves with some of the principles of hermeneutics, it should become easier for us to break through the barriers of time, geography, culture, and language. Then we can more faithfully grasp the message of the Bible and apply it in our lives today.

2

Interpreters
and the Bible

Anyone interested in the study of the Word of God must have access to the Holy Scriptures. That's not a problem in the Western world, where most people can afford a Bible. But there are still multitudes of Christians who do not own a Bible. Many people in the early church did not have a copy of the Scriptures either; handwritten copies were expensive to produce. However, they *heard* the Word of God as it was read to them when they gathered for worship.

Thus Paul tells Timothy to "give attention to the public reading of scripture" (1 Tim. 4:13). The last book of the Bible begins with a beatitude upon "the one who reads aloud the words of the prophecy." It then pronounces a blessing upon "those who hear and keep what is written in it" (Rev. 1:3).

For serious study of the Word of God, however, we need to have a Bible. But simply owning a Bible does not yet give us access to the message of the Scriptures; we must also be able to read. In our society, where education is compulsory, we assume that all people can read, but some cannot and many are poor readers. In many areas of the world, the situation is even worse. In the sixteenth-century period of Tyndale, known as the

Father of the English Bible, England was still largely illiterate. The publication of Bibles in English accelerated the growth of literacy.

Hence, fundamental prerequisites for understanding the written Word of God are (1) possession of a Bible in a language the reader can understand, and (2) the ability to read. Since, however, the Scriptures are divinely inspired, we also need (3) spiritual help if we are to understand the message of the Bible.

Moreover, we need (4) awareness of our own pre-understandings that we bring to the Bible, lest we read into the Bible what isn't there. We want to look at several of these aspects of Bible study that concern both interpreters and the Bible.

Literary Skill

Since the Bible is literature, we at least need some literary expertise if we are to hear its message. Every area of investigation requires the appropriate tools to do the job. A scientist needs the microscope, test tubes, a telescope, a computer, and other equipment. Such tools are helpful for studying the heavens or probing the secrets of human genes. They are, however, of little help when we seek to understand the Scriptures. When dealing with literature, we have to have literary equipment.

For the specialist, this will mean acquaintance with the original languages of the Bible—Hebrew, Aramaic, and Greek. Most Bible readers, however, study the Scriptures in one or more translations or versions. That is okay if the translators were careful to preserve the meanings of the original languages. Already several hundred years before Christ, Alexandrian Jews read their Bible in a Greek translation (the Septuagint). The NT books were written in Greek, but it wasn't long before the NT was translated into Syriac, Old Latin, and other languages, for people who did not read Greek.

The Western church, from the fourth century to the time of the Protestant Reformation, read the Bible primarily in a Latin translation. The medieval church, in fact, discouraged the translation of the Bible into modern languages. The church hierarchy was afraid people might develop wrong ideas if they read the Bible in their mother tongue. Roman Catholics today, happily, have the freedom to read good modern translations.

Bible scholars are expected to know the original languages of Scripture. They have studied ancient history, are informed on the geography of the Mediterranean world, and know something about the political systems in the days when the biblical books were written. Such readers are obviously better equipped to explore the Scriptures. Mature Christians do not view expertise in these and other areas of knowledge as against the Christian faith.

There is no minimum educational requirement for Bible study, but students have to be able to read—or at least have a good memory if listening to Scripture being read. A familiarity with other literature greatly enhances our ability to read the Bible. If, for example, we have an appreciation for poetry, we will find it easier to understand the many figures of speech in the Bible.

Literary equipment alone, however, will not suffice in our efforts to capture the message of the Bible. Since we are studying a book that deals with messages from God, we will also need spiritual equipment. That is the only way we can hear what God is saying to us in the books of the Bible.

Spiritual Helps

Although a knowledge of grammar is an absolute necessity for Bible study, it is not enough. The scribes of

Jesus' day were experts in the reading of the Scriptures and in the details of Hebrew grammar, but they somehow failed to hear God's word. "You search the scriptures," says Jesus, "because you think that in them you have eternal life; and it is they that testify on my behalf. Yet you refuse to come to me to have life" (John 5:39-40).

To understand an inspired record, the interpreter must have the same Spirit that enabled the prophets and apostles, who wrote the books of the Bible, to receive their messages from God. "Those who are unspiritual," writes Paul, "do not receive the gifts of God's Spirit, for they are foolishness to them, and they are unable to understand them because they are spiritually discerned" (1 Cor. 2:14).

When Paul says that the things of God are foolishness to those who do not have the Spirit of God, he does not mean that unbelievers cannot understand the words of Scripture. Non-Christians can arrive at the correct mental grasp of the meaning of a biblical text. If that were not so, people could not come to know Christ through the reading of the Word of God. But readers who understand the words and sentences do not necessarily grasp the message of the Bible.

Without the help of the Spirit of God, unbelieving readers fail to hear and to accept the message of the gospel. They miss God's invitation to put their faith in the finished work of Christ.

Hermann Menge was a German philologist who knew and taught ancient languages. To his own embarrassment, he acknowledged that in his teaching career he had never bothered reading the NT. When he retired from teaching, he decided to read through the Greek NT. When reading ancient literature, he customarily made his own translation into German.

This intimate conversation with the Word of God

transformed his life, and he became a humble follower of Christ. He went on to translate the Hebrew OT as well. Eventually, in 1926, the entire Menge Bible was published. He had come to realize that his linguistic expertise did not yet unlock the message of the Bible. The Holy Spirit had to open his eyes.

J. B. Phillips, an Englishman, had a similar experience during World War II. In 1940, he was reading the NT to frightened young people sitting in bunkers during the German blitz. The King James English (of the 1611 Bible) did not make an impact on these teenagers, who had never been to church. So he began reading his translations for them. When he saw their response, he was encouraged to turn book after book into contemporary English. His version became *The New Testament in Modern English* (1958).

In the process of translating the NT, his own life was transformed. When he worked through the book of Acts, he says, he felt like an electrician rewiring an old house without being able to turn off the current. He discovered he was working with literature that was "alive." Phillips learned that if he was to capture the message of the NT books, he needed to be in tune with the writers.

We need the help of the Spirit of God to understand what God is saying to us in the Scriptures. Paul explains that "the god of this world has blinded the minds of the unbelievers" (2 Cor. 4:4). He says that unbelieving Jews have a veil over their minds; only when they turn to the Lord is that veil removed (2 Cor. 3:15-16). We need a spiritual antenna to receive the waves of eternity.

A famous German NT scholar Adolf Schlatter (of Tübingen) used to tell his theology students that they could not read. They could read the words, of course; they could read even the Greek texts. But what he meant was that they were not hearing what God was saying to them in these texts. They couldn't read "between the lines," as he put it.

To understand the Bible, we must come with hearts that are humble, repentant, prayerful, and willing to obey God's Word. In *Pensées,* Blaise Pascal observed that divine things, if they are to be understood, must first be loved.

A Danish theologian Søren Kierkegaard suggested that the Bible be read like love letters. People read them over and over and read between the lines. Love letters, he said, are really understood only by the recipient of the letters, who stands in a loving relationship with the writer.

Kierkegaard criticized the theologians of his day, who stressed the importance of grammatical historical study of the Bible. They were, he claimed, like the schoolboy who had been naughty and who knew he would get whipped. So he prepared himself for the ordeal by stuffing his pockets with dictionaries and grammars. He would then not feel the sting of the rod quite so keenly. In similar fashion, said Kierkegaard, some theologians couldn't hear what God was saying in his Word because they had barricaded themselves behind grammars and dictionaries.

This is not to suggest, however, that the help of the Holy Spirit is a substitute for literary skill. The Spirit does not teach us the rules of grammar. The Spirit does not give us information on history, geography, culture, and the like. Neither does personal piety guarantee correct understanding of the Bible. We must come to the Scriptures in a spirit of prayer, but prayer as such is not a method of interpretation.

Professor Donald Carson, of Trinity Evangelical Divinity School, tells of a fellow believer who shared with him what God had told him on the basis of a particular passage. Carson noticed immediately that he had misread the text and gently suggested that the passage may be saying something else.

"But the Holy Spirit does not lie," the man replied.

Carson asked, "What would you say if I claimed that the Holy Spirit tells me something else when I read that verse?"

"Then, I suppose, God says different things to different people." He could not admit that his reading of the text might be at fault. After all, he had God's Spirit in his heart. When Jesus promised that the coming Spirit would lead his followers into all truth (John 16:13), he meant that with the Spirit's help they would be able to grasp what God had done in Christ. Jesus did not mean that the Spirit would do the exegesis (explanation) of the biblical text for them, or that the Spirit would give them revelations on par with Scripture.

Prayer is not an exegetical method, either. It puts us into the right attitude toward God, so that we are open to receive instruction from God's Word, but it is not a means of explaining a passage. Unbelievers also are able to read the biblical texts and understand the grammatical import of a passage. But as long as they reject God's message, they cannot really grasp the significance of what God is saying.

Years ago, a German professor named Kopfwissen gave a lecture on Paul's doctrine of justification by faith. He made it clear to his audience what Paul meant by *justification*. Paul would have been thankful, had he been in the audience, to hear the professor interpreting the apostle correctly and lucidly.

The lecture ended with applause from the hearers. Professor Kopfwissen responded, "But you know, of course, that it's all humbug." This man could expound biblical texts grammatically, without hearing what the Spirit was saying. He recognized the meaning of the text but was not willing to live by it. He knew the meaning of justification by faith, but it held no personal significance for him.

In biblical hermeneutics, obedience to the Word of God is another important element in the process of interpretation. A Bible reader who is interested only in what the text means, without any intention of doing what it asks of the reader, will be greatly handicapped in grasping the true significance of the text. Hans Denck, a sixteenth-century Anabaptist pioneer, put it this way: "No one can truly know Christ except the one who follows Christ in daily life."

Interpreters, as we have seen, need literary equipment to interpret the Bible, and they need help from above. In addition, interpreters need to be aware of their own pre-understandings of the Bible.

Pre-Understandings

Every Bible reader brings a body of assumptions and attitudes to the Scriptures. No one approaches the Bible in a totally objective manner. We come to the Word of God with our beliefs, experiences, prejudices, and needs. Christians read the NT in the light of their faith; Jews may read the NT with respect or suspicion; agnostics expect to ridicule it or find it to be a stumbling block. Even professional NT experts may wear blinders or shades as they approach the text.

To state it figuratively, we all read the Bible through our own colored glasses. Most of the time, we are not conscious of our pre-understandings, but they are always there. Our situation in life varies a great deal: when we are in sorrow, we ask different questions of the Bible than when we are glad. Children listen with a different ear to God's Word than do grownups.

In retrospect, we can see more readily how pre-understandings on the part of leading interpreters have influenced them as they read the biblical texts. The great third-century scholar Origen (of Alexandria) tended to interpret the Bible in the light of philosophical assumptions borrowed from ancient Greek thinkers.

The nineteenth-century German professor F. C. Baur (of Tübingen) interpreted the NT largely on the basis of Hegel's three-stage philosophy (*thesis:* Jewish Christianity; *antithesis:* Hellenistic Christianity; *synthesis:* catholic Christianity). More recently, Rudolf Bultmann applied his existentialist philosophy to the interpretation of the NT, and thus rejected miracles in the Gospels.

In 1906 Albert Schweitzer published a German book translated in 1910 as *The Quest of the Historical Jesus.* In it he reviews many volumes on who Jesus was. In the end he concludes that most of the portraits of Jesus drawn by these many authors were reflections of their own image.

Schweitzer compares the authors to a man who looks into a deep well and in the water below he sees a face. He decides to sketch this image, not realizing that he is drawing the reflection of his own face. Some have portrayed Jesus as a friend of children, a lover of nature, or an outdoorsman; still others, as a Jewish prophet, as a political revolutionary, as an ascetic, as a superstar, as a capitalist, or as a socialist, and the like.

In his day, Martin Luther warned, the gospel should not be treated like a wax nose that we can shape as we wish. Yet this is precisely what has happened repeatedly in history.

Some Protestants still find it hard to read Matthew 16:18, where Jesus says, "You are Peter, and on this rock I will build my church, and the gates of Hades will not prevail against it." Usually they seek an interpretation that does not give Peter the significance the Roman Catholic Church has given him.

Third John 2 is a favorite among those who espouse the popular health-and-wealth doctrine. Here John prays that Gaius might be in good physical health, to match the health of his soul. But in no way does the text guarantee that those with healthy souls will also be healthy in body and wealthy.

Oral Roberts, in his book *How I Learned Jesus Was Not Poor*, invites people to read his book and promises that they will never be poor again. Whoever brings to a text misfitting theological presuppositions from elsewhere is bound to read it incorrectly.

When in graduate school, I enrolled in a course to study Hebrews. This epistle is full of warnings to Christian readers not to become indifferent or to fall away from the faith. The professor knew the text thoroughly. He encountered constant resistance from students who had grown up in the Calvinist tradition, which taught that believers are eternally secure against apostasy. They argued that the readers of Hebrews could, therefore, not have been Christians.

The professor, however, repeatedly reminded them that their problem was not the epistle to the Hebrews but their dogmatic theology. They were trying to interpret Hebrews, with all of its warnings, through the grid of their Calvinistic upbringing.

Our pre-understanding often leads us to select passages supporting our interpretation of the Scriptures and to overlook those pointing in a different direction. Some hold that women should be free in the church to perform any service they are able to do; they will usually argue from Galatians 3:28, "There is no longer male and female; for all of you are one in Christ Jesus."

Others argue from 1 Timothy 2:12 that Paul puts some restrictions on women: "I permit no woman to teach or to have authority over a man." We must take both passages seriously. The church must find a way to respect both of these emphases (Swartley, 1983).

Dispensationalism is a popular grid through which many read the Bible today. This system of interpretation maintains that Jesus came to establish a kingdom for Israel, which didn't work out. Hence, the teachings of Jesus about the kingdom do not really apply to the church. The Sermon on the Mount represents the laws of the coming millennial kingdom. Since the Jews rejected Christ, the kingdom was postponed, Dispensationalists say.

Through Christ's death and resurrection and the outpouring of the Spirit, God then established the church. Dispensationalists claim that when the church is raptured, God will establish the kingdom for Israel. *The Scofield Reference Bible* mentions other aspects of Dispensationalism.

We can readily see that when people accept such a theological system, they read the Bible through this grid and press texts to fit it. This is a Procrustean bed, named after the Greek mythological figure Procrustes, who trimmed or stretched his visitors to fit his guest bed. Similarly, such interpreters chop up the Bible or add doctrines to fit their system.

Our pre-understandings are often influenced by our times. Around 1900, postmillennialism was a widely held view, holding that a golden age will come on this earth before the return of Christ at the end of history. This teaching reflected an optimistic but shallow view of human history. People expected Christianity to spread all over the world. They thought wars would soon be a thing of the past. The reign of God, hopefully, would soon be acknowledged universally.

Then came World War I and World War II. Communism spread, and Islam threatened the Christian church. Today such a triumphalistic postmillennialism is no longer a widely held view. It is another illustration of how attitudes influence people when they read the Scriptures.

Jürgen Moltmann, a well-known German theologian, wrote some years ago: "Because I am not an angel, but a human being, my perspectives are limited. They are European and Protestant, Western and middle class; they arise out of the 20th century . . . and, finally, they are determined by my personal experiences and private limitations" (*Evangelisches Missionsmagazin* 118:1015).

Not all Bible readers are willing to admit that they have pre-understandings when they try to understand the Scriptures. We may not always be conscious of them, but they are always there. Those familiar with the history of interpretation can often easily detect the source of some of their theological views.

Once some African church leaders and some Western missionaries agreed to study the Joseph stories for their daily devotions at a conference. At the end of the meetings, everyone tackled a question: "What might be the main lesson that we can take with us from our studies of Joseph's life?"

The Western missionaries suggested that it was Joseph's faithfulness to God, regardless of the circumstances into which he was thrown. The African leaders thought otherwise: It was rather Joseph's faithfulness to his family; wherever he went, he never forgot his family. Here a difference in cultural outlook had clearly influenced the pre-understanding of the Bible readers.

Is there then no escape from our subjective approach to the biblical text? Not really. But if we are willing to acknowledge that we all have pre-understandings, then we will be extra careful in reading the Bible. We want to make sure that we are not reading our own prejudices into it. This means that we must always be open to correction when we read the Scriptures. We want to avoid errors that can come from an individualistic reading of the Bible. Hence, it is important for us to test our understandings of the Scriptures in the community of the saints, the church.

As stated in the *Confession of Faith in a Mennonite Perspective*, "The Bible is the essential book of the church. Through the Bible, the Holy Spirit nurtures the obedience of faith to Jesus Christ and guides the church in shaping its teaching, witnessing, and worship" (22). Within the community of the saints, individual insights and interpretations of Scripture need to be tested. God's Spirit working in the church will help us understand the text inspired by that same Spirit (1 Cor. 14:26-33; 1 Thess. 5:21; 2 Pet. 1:20-21).

3

The Uniqueness of the Sacred Scriptures

Protestant biblical hermeneutics confines itself to the interpretation of the thirty-nine OT and the twenty-seven NT books. These books form the Protestant canon.

The word *canon* is a Semitic word meaning "reed" or "stalk." It came to denote a rule, a measuring stick, or an instrument with which to make straight lines. Metaphorically, it is used for any standard, whether in art, music, literature, or morals. The word *canon* eventually came to be used for the list of books that the church accepted as belonging to the Holy Scriptures.

Roman Catholics hold to a wider canon than Protestants. Hence, we need to say something about the Protestant canon setting the parameters for our hermeneutical work.

Sadly, some in the Protestant tradition want to accept books beyond the canon as authoritative. They have difficulty accepting clearly defined boundary lines between the Scriptures and other religious literature. Among Evangelicals, however, it is understood that the Bible consists of sixty-six books in two collections, called Testaments or Covenants.

Since Bible readers often ask why certain books are

in the Bible and others not, it may be helpful to say a few things about the Protestant canon.

The Protestant Canon of Scripture

Christian Bible readers have less difficulty accepting the limits of the OT collection of sacred books than those of the NT. After all, Jesus and his apostles viewed the books of the Old Covenant as God's Word. By the time of Jesus, the OT books had been collected into three parts: the Law, the Prophets, and the Writings.

Jesus refers to this three-part collection in his conversation with the Emmaus disciples: "the law of Moses, the prophets, and the psalms" (Luke 24:44). Since the Psalms often stood at the head of the Writings, the entire division was sometimes called "the Psalms."

We do not need to discuss at length the process by which the OT collection of sacred books was formed. Content, chronology, liturgy, and other factors played a role in the formation of the OT. Some ancient Jewish scholars asked why the canon should include books such as Esther, Song of Solomon, Ecclesiastes, and a few others. Yet the Hebrew canon of twenty-four books (divided into thirty-nine in our Bibles) was generally accepted in Judaism before the apostolic period and was endorsed by Jesus and the apostles.

Modern Bible readers often wonder, though, whether the so-called Apocrypha should be read as sacred Scripture or not, especially since these books are often included in some editions of the Bible. How they got into the Greek translation of the OT is not quite clear; they were never part of the Hebrew Bible.

The books of the Apocrypha are a valuable source of information about Jewish life and thought before the Christian era. The Roman Catholic hierarchy, at the Council of Trent (1546), declared them to be of equal authority with the other books of the Bible, but Protestants disagreed.

On the question as to whether or not the books of the Apocrypha should be accepted as canonical, the following considerations may help.

First, they never were part of the Hebrew canon.

Second, though the NT has allusions to the Apocrypha, Jesus and his apostles did not base important teachings on these books.

Third, in the sermons of the apostles, recorded in the book of Acts, the speakers repeatedly review the history of salvation. They start with Abraham, David, or some other OT worthy, and end with the coming of Christ, but always skip over the centuries between the last book of the Hebrew Bible and Christ's coming. Yet the Apocryphal books tell us much about that period.

Fourth, there has always been uncertainty about whether these books are authoritative, and that is not something that can be said about the other OT books. The church did not sense them to bear the stamp of God like the books that now belong to the canon. They were not as true a guide to God's purposes.

For these and other reasons, Protestants have not given canonical status to the OT Apocrypha. Bruce M. Metzger writes, "When one compares the books of the Apocrypha with the books of the OT, the impartial reader must conclude that, as a whole, the true greatness of the canonical books is clearly apparent" (1957:172).

The question of the NT canon is somewhat more complicated. There were many other Christian books in circulation during the period in which the NT canon was formed. By the end of the first century, all the books that now comprise our NT had been written. However, at first they circulated individually or in smaller collections in the larger centers of Christianity.

In the earlier collections, several of the shorter General Epistles were missing. In the Western church, the epistle to the Hebrews was absent for a long time. In the Greek-speaking Eastern church, the book of Revelation was not accepted for some time. The Syriac-speaking church, in the Land of the Two Rivers (Mesopotamia), for several centuries did without the General Epistles. But as time went by, all the twenty-seven books of the NT were accepted universally in the church.

Our confession of faith is that the Spirit of God led the churches to acknowledge these books as the Word of God. Yet in retrospect we can say that there were a number of factors guiding the church in the formation of the NT canon.

First, there was the matter of *apostolicity*. The apostles were regarded as men who had been uniquely in the confidence of Jesus. They had been eyewitnesses of the Christ event. So the church accepted only those books that had the authority of the apostles behind them.

Behind Luke, whose writings comprise about a quarter of the entire NT, stood the authority of Paul. Behind Mark, also not a member of the twelve apostles, stood the authority of Peter. Even when the names of apostolic authors are not mentioned in several of the NT books, it was significant that they were apostolic in content.

Second, there was what some of the church fathers called *the rule of faith*. This was not a document, but a digest of apostolic teaching found in the churches established by the apostles. This essential content of the Christian faith was helpful in combating heresy and in determining whether a book was apostolic in content or not. By itself this would have been an insufficient guide, for there were other Christian writings that were orthodox in teaching. Yet it is one of a number of elements that went into the formation of the NT canon.

A *third* criterion for canonicity was its universal acceptance, called its *catholicity*. A document acknowledged as Scripture only in a small corner of Christianity was unlikely ever to gain acceptance as the Word of God.

Fourth, the matter of *chronology* also played a role in the determination of which books belonged to the canon. Oscar Cullmann points out that only books that belong to the "period of the incarnation" were considered as authoritative for the church (77). By the period of the incarnation, he means the apostolic age. Christian books written at a later period, though they may be in harmony with the teaching of the apostles, do not belong to the canon.

The epistle of Jude may be less interesting than Bunyan's *Pilgrim's Progress*. But Jude is an apostolic witness, while Bunyan is not. Chronology obviously overlaps with apostolicity.

Fifth, there is also the *self-evidencing quality* of the NT books. These books had the stamp of God upon them. They did not become sacred Scripture because they were accepted into the canon. Instead, they were accepted into the canon because they were recognized as inspired writings.

When these books were read, the Spirit in the hearts of believers gave witness to the word of God and built them up in faith and obedience. Though 2 Timothy 3:16-17 refers to the OT, Christians believe the same principles of being inspired and useful apply to the NT.

Before printing made the Bible widely available, few Christians owned a complete collection of these sacred writings. Yet in the worship services of the church, they heard God speaking to them. We know that several other Christian writings were read in some churches in the days when the NT canon was emerging, but they were eventually excluded.

Floyd Filson writes that the twenty-seven books of the NT "were preserved in living touch with the church, and they received their unique place only because they proved in continued practice and throughout the entire church that they could bring home the gospel with ever new appeal and power" (128).

In the early centuries of the Christian era, there were several attempts either to reduce or to expand the NT canon. Eventually the church accepted only the twenty-seven books as we have them in our NT. Hermeneutics is about the process of grasping the message of these OT and NT books. In this endeavor, we need to discover the basic message of the Bible.

The Basic Message of the Bible

Some years ago an Oxford professor asked a number of biblical scholars to state briefly their views of the fundamental message of the Bible. The answers were not all given in the same form, but there was general agreement that the Bible is *salvation history*, or *Heilsgeschichte,* as the Germans say.

If this had been recognized sufficiently in the history of interpretation, believers might have been spared a lot of grief. Too often the Bible is viewed somewhat like an encyclopedia and is expected to give answers to questions it doesn't really address.

When we read a book, it makes a big difference whether it is a book on history, philosophy, science, or mathematics. We would not think of addressing religious questions to a book on physics. But when we read the Bible, we certainly ask religious questions of it.

The Bible was not written to open up for us the mysteries of biology, but to speak to the problems of sin and suffering, life and death, and our relationships with God and each other.

Some of the long conflict between scientists and theologians might have been avoided if people had recognized more clearly that the Scriptures are concerned primarily with our salvation. Galileo (1564-1643) by his experiments concluded that the earth turns around the sun, rather than the sun around the earth, as in the Ptolemaic system of thought.

The established church opposed Galileo on the grounds that his views were against the Bible. But he was seeking to discover "how the heavens go," and not "how to go to heaven." The Inquisition, however, forbade him from teaching that the sun is in the center of our solar system.

Natural scientists often go beyond their fields of inquiry and make judgments on what are essentially theological questions. Theologians have sometimes misused the Bible by trying to make it speak in the accents of modern science.

The Genesis account of creation has come to us in a form that remains meaningful for Christians of all ages. It answers theological questions about the origin and purpose of all things and provides the stage for the story Adam and Eve. They were created and then fell into sin (Gen. 1–3). From there, the Bible tells us what God does to deliver humankind from sin and eternal death, and to call them together in covenant with God.

That doesn't mean that we do not have a great deal of valuable information in the Bible on other subjects, particularly on the history of Israel. But the basic message of the entire biblical canon is that "God so loved the world that he gave his only Son, so that everyone who believes in him may not perish but may have eternal life" (John 3:16).

The prophets and the apostles, who received messages from God, were keenly aware of the limits of their knowledge. Paul confesses that "we know only in part" (1 Cor. 13:9), and the apostle John reminds the readers of Revelation that he is passing on to them "all that he saw" (Rev. 1:2). What they saw is trustworthy, but they too had questions that will be answered only in eternity.

Hence, we should not pretend to be wiser than the apostles. It is much better to acknowledge our ignorance about subjects not addressed in the Bible, than to make the Bible into an encyclopedia for producing easy answers.

This means that Christians will often disagree on certain doctrinal and ethical questions, simply because the Scriptures do not address them directly. On one basic question all Bible readers do agree: the Scriptures are the good news of our salvation. That agreement gives believers a foundation for further dialogue and decision making.

Someone has compared the Bible to the headlights of a motorcar. These lights enable us to drive in the dark. Drivers will safely reach their destination if they stay on the road illuminated by the headlights. If they get too interested in the landscape that lies beyond the light, they will surely land in the ditch.

The Bible provides every honest reader with enough light for the present life and the life to come, but it doesn't illuminate the entire landscape of human inquiry and knowledge. This understanding affects the goal of hermeneutics.

The Goal of Interpretation

There is a place for the academic investigation of the biblical books. Yet the ultimate goal of Bible study is not simply to establish what an ancient author meant to say. Paul expressed the purpose of God's Word in this way: "All scripture is inspired by God and is useful for teaching, for reproof, for correction, and for training in righteousness, so that everyone who belongs to God may be proficient, equipped for every good work" (2 Tim. 3:16-17).

The Bible is to be applied to our lives. Its purpose is to shape our thinking, call us to our task here on earth, encourage us when we are distressed, teach us how to live, and give us hope for the world to come.

By comparison, if we read a history of the Napoléonic wars, we make no effort to apply it to our daily lives. Believers who read the Bible, however, constantly ask, What is God saying to us and to me through this passage? Hence, the vital usefulness and benefit of the Scriptures makes them unique.

4

Languages and Translations of the Bible

The confusion of languages at the tower of Babel was God's judgment on people who were rejecting human limitations and seeking fame and unity, but apart from fellowship with God (Gen. 11: 1-9).

At Pentecost, by contrast, God broke through the language barriers, as an act of grace (Acts 2). Thousands of visitors from all over the Roman world heard the good news of salvation in their native dialects.

By breaking down language barriers on the day of Pentecost, God was telling the church that its mission in the world has a similar purpose: to bring the gospel to people speaking different languages.

The early church took this calling seriously and translated the NT into ancient Syriac and (Old) Latin. Other versions followed, in Egyptian languages, Ethiopic, Armenian, Georgian, and even Gothic. This was the first wave of translation. Thus, although many people still could not read, these versions enabled them to hear the Scriptures read in their native languages.

In the Middle Ages, from 500 to 1500, hardly anyone was translating the Bible. The Western church had Jerome's Latin Vulgate (originating in the fourth to fifth centuries) and did not encourage translations into other tongues. Yet during this period, most people in the West did not understand much Latin.

With the Protestant Reformation in the sixteenth century, however, we find the second wave of biblical translation. Bibles appeared in Dutch, French, English, German, and other languages. The development of the printing press made them more generally available.

Some of these translations, such as the English, were first made at great risk. The Roman Catholic Church persecuted those presenting the Scriptures in modern languages so laypeople could study them. The Catholic hierarchy claimed that it alone had the right to give proper interpretations of the Bible. They tried to protect their position by keeping the Bible in Latin (see chap. 8).

Without these new translations, however, we can hardly imagine the Reformation that took place in the sixteenth century. Many people again had access to the Bible in their native languages; they could hear it read, understand the words, and even learn to read it themselves. When they were able to read and study the Bible, the effect was dramatic.

The twentieth century, in spite of wars, famines, and other catastrophes, represents a third wave in Bible translation. Today believers in all the countries of the world have access to at least a portion of the Bible in their mother tongue. Modern linguistic science has helped to accelerate the annual rate of Scripture translation work.

For us, however, it is important to remember that the Bible was originally written in Hebrew, Aramaic, and Greek. Hence, every translation of the original texts into other languages is in part also an interpretation of these texts. Hermeneutics, therefore, cannot be divorced from translation. Indeed, the word *hermeneutics* means both translation and interpretation. Languages represent unique ways of thinking. We should, therefore, explain some things about the languages in which the Bible was originally written.

Hebrew

Most of the OT was written in the Hebrew language. There is nothing sacred about this language; it just happened to be the language spoken by the people of Israel to whom God had chosen to make himself known.

Hebrew belongs to a large family of Semitic languages. The ancestors of the Israelites apparently spoke Aramaic. When Abraham and his clan settled in Canaan, they evidently picked up elements of the local Canaanite language. Eventually the Israelites moved to Egypt, where they lived in relative isolation for 430 years. Yet some Egyptian words were incorporated into the language that came to be called Hebrew.

This Hebrew was the language Israel brought back to Canaan, although differences in dialect and pronunciation tended to develop between tribes living on the east side of Jordan and those on the west (as in Judg. 12:6). By the time Judah went into exile in Babylon (586 B.C.), the transition from Hebrew to Aramaic had begun.

Aramaic

Aramaic is also a Semitic language and thus related to Hebrew. It was the language of Syria and gained international use in the Near East from the seventh century B.C. (2 Kings 18:26). While the Jews lived in exile in Mesopotamia, they adopted Aramaic as their everyday language. This explains why large portions of Daniel and Ezra are written in Aramaic.

When some of the exiles returned to Judea under Persian rule, they spoke Aramaic and had some difficulty in understanding the Hebrew books of the Bible, as Nehemiah 8:8 illustrates. It became necessary, therefore, to have a translator turn the Hebrew text orally into Aramaic in their meetings and in the synagogue.

Aramaic was the everyday language of Jesus and his apostles. A number of Aramaic words and phrases have been retained even in the Greek NT, such as *talitha cum, ephphatha, Abba, Marana tha* (Mark 5:41; 7:34; Rom. 8:15; 1 Cor. 16:22). Aramaic continued to be spoken even after Greek became the common language of the Mediterranean world.

By the beginning of the Christian era, Aramaic had split into two branches, West Aramaic and East Aramaic. East Aramaic became the language of the Syriac-speaking church in Mesopotamia. Even in Palestine there were slight differences between the way people spoke Aramaic in Galilee and the way they spoke in Judea (Matt. 26:73).

Greek

God's final revelation in Christ, to which the apostles bear witness, was recorded in Greek. Through the conquests of Alexander the Great, the Greek language spread to all the lands surrounding the Mediterranean.

With the breakup of Alexander's empire, Rome extended its rule over the then-known world. As a result, Latin became the language of law, the military, and the government. However, Greek was still spoken all over the empire. It was in this "world language" that the books of the NT came to be written.

Greek was spoken in ancient Greece. But the NT books were written not in classical Greek but in Hellenistic Greek, called Koiné (common) Greek. This made sense because it was the common language used from the fourth century B.C. *and* had absorbed several

Greek dialects from earlier times.

From the fourth century A.D. till the fall of Constantinople in 1453, we have the period of Byzantine Greek. After the Byzantine empire comes the period of Modern Greek, still spoken in Greece.

Most of the writers of the Greek NT were Jews. Their Greek was influenced by the Hebrew of the OT and by the Aramaic commonly spoken in Palestine at the time of Jesus.

Latin, the language of the ruling power, Rome, also influenced the Greek of the NT. Some of the monetary and military terms are simply from Latin.

When quoting the OT, the writers of the NT mostly used a translation into Greek that Alexandrian Jews had made as early as the third century B.C. This Greek version of the OT, known as the Septuagint, served as a bridge between the two Testaments.

Important Ancient Versions

Once the books of the NT were written, it did not take long before they too were translated from the Greek into several other ancient languages.

The book of Acts gives us some glimpses of the gospel moving to the west; we know less about its movement to the east. However, already by the second century, there was a dynamic Syriac-speaking church in Mesopotamia. The Syriac used by Christians is Aramaic written with a different set of letters.

Jews living in this region may have already begun to turn parts of the OT into Syriac before the coming of Christianity.

In any case, by the year 170, a Christian named Tatian had produced what came to be known as the Diatessaron (through the four). He took the four Gospels and made one unified account out of them. This "mixed" Gospel became so popular that it was translated into many other languages.

In Syriac, the "unmixed" Gospels appeared side by side with this "mixed" one. Eventually there emerged the Peshitta (simple, common). It included all the books of the NT except the General Epistles and Revelation and became the standard Syriac Version.

Although people in Alexandria and its environs spoke Greek, Christians living in regions farther south along the Nile spoke Coptic dialects, such as Bohairic and Sahidic. As early as the third century, believers started to translate the NT into these languages. These versions were produced in the missionary ventures of Egyptian Christianity.

This was also the case with the Armenian version, and indeed with nearly all the ancient versions of the Scriptures. Armenia likely received the gospel from Syriac missionaries as early as the third century. For the Armenian version, as for several other ancient ones, translators first had to devise alphabets.

North of Armenia lay Georgia, in the Caucusus Mountains. By mid fifth century, the Gospels were available in Georgian, and the other books were translated later.

There is evidence that the Christian faith had come to Ethiopia by the end of the fourth century. By the end of the fifth century, almost the entire country had been Christianized. This led to the translation of parts of the Bible into Old Ethiopic, called Ge'ez. The Ethiopic Bible contains some books (such as First Enoch and Jubilees) not found in our Protestant Bibles but counted in the pseudepigrapha (Charlesworth).

In the first two centuries of the Christian era, the Roman church spoke mostly Greek. By the beginning of the third century, it began changing to Latin. This was a slow process, and several bilingual manuscripts of Scripture portions reflect this transition from Greek to Latin.

From the second century, the earliest translations of the Bible into Latin evidently were made in the Roman province of Africa. Christianity flourished there in the early centuries. There were parallel efforts also in Italy.

The various Old Latin attempts at translating the Scriptures led to some confusion. Hence, in the fourth century, Pope Damasus decided to bring some order out of this chaos. He called upon one of the most learned men of his day, Jerome, to produce a new Latin Bible.

Jerome's translation came to be known as the Vulgate (common, popular), but it did not immediately supplant all the older Latin versions. Nevertheless, the Latin Vulgate became the Bible of Western Christianity for a thousand years, up to the time of the Renaissance and the Reformation.

Though Jerome was hesitant about translating the OT Apocrypha, he yielded to pressure, and these Jewish books became part of the Vulgate. The Roman Catholic Church eventually declared them to be canonical (Council of Trent, 1546). Beginning in 1566, many Catholic scholars have called them deuterocanonical, "later added to the canon."

North of the Danube lived the Goths. The Christian faith came to this region as well. The man who gave the Goths the Scriptures in their mother tongue was Ulfilas (Gothic: "little wolf"). A parchment leaf of a bilingual codex, with Gothic on one side and Latin on the other, came to light in Egypt in 1908.

About the middle of the ninth century, a Moravian empire was formed in Eastern Europe, professing Christianity. Slavonic-speaking priests from Byzantium, Constantine (later named Cyril), and Methodius went to work in this region. Like many translators before them, they devised an alphabet, this time Cyrillic for the Slavonic language. They translated the Scriptures from Greek into Slavonic.

This survey of ancient versions shows us that in the early centuries of the Christian era, churches read and studied the Bible mainly in translations. That is true also in the English-speaking world today.

English Translations

The gospel came to England in the early centuries of the Christian era. Yet England had no Bible until Roman Catholic missionaries brought the Latin Vulgate there at the end of the sixth century. Several attempts were then made to translate small portions of the Latin Bible into Anglo-Saxon at a time when England was largely illiterate.

In the fourteenth century, John Wycliffe made the first complete translation of the Bible into Middle English. This was before the day of printing, so copies were written by hand. The Roman Church fiercely opposed Wycliffe's efforts to give English people a Bible in their language, and his followers were persecuted. Hence, Wycliffe is called "the morning star of the Reformation."

Although Wycliffe was a pioneer, he was not the "father" of the English Bible. That honor goes to William Tyndale, who translated the Scriptures from the original Hebrew and Greek into English. He did his work on the European continent because it was too dangerous to do it in England. By 1526 copies of his translation were smuggled into England and circulated. By this time, printing had been developed, and Tyndale's translations appeared in print. Tyndale was persecuted and burned at the stake outside of Antwerp in 1536. His last words have been reported: "O Lord, open the King of England's eyes."

Miles Coverdale had worked with Tyndale on the continent and published an English version in 1535. By that time Henry VIII had broken with Rome. He gave permission for people to circulate Coverdale's version in England. Another version, prepared by John Rogers (pen name: Thomas Matthew), also was circulated. However, there was as yet no version authorized by the king.

However, with the publication of the Great Bible in 1539, the English clergy were ordered to place a copy in every church. When Henry VIII's reign came to an end in 1547, England reverted to Catholicism. Copies of English Bibles were burned, and so were translators; John Rogers died at the stake.

Under Mary I (1553-58), many Protestant scholars left England to escape persecution. Some settled in Geneva, and here they produced what came to be called the Geneva Bible in 1560. When Elizabeth I took the throne, this version was taken to England and became quite popular. It was the Bible of Shakespeare, of the Puritans, and of the Pilgrim Fathers.

When James I became king of England in 1603, he was asked to authorize an English translation of the Bible that would be used by all English churches. The king agreed and played a role in getting the project organized. Some of the finest biblical scholars of England, including several Puritans, completed their task in 1611.

For more than 350 years, this English version has retained its hold on many Bible readers. Like all new translations, it encountered sharp criticism when it first appeared. Eventually it became the household Bible of English people all over the world.

As time passed, changes took place:
- More ancient manuscripts were discovered.
- Scholars improved their understanding of the vocabulary and grammar of the biblical languages.
- The English language kept changing.

These three developments eventually led to calls for a thorough revision of the King James Version (known also as the Authorized Version).

Such a revision was carried through in 1881 to 1885. This English Revised Version was an accurate translation, but it never gained the popularity of the King James Version. American scholars in 1901 published the American Standard Version, which did become quite popular in America. A revision appeared in 1970 as the New American Standard Version.

Between 1611 and the twentieth century, many translations of the Bible into English were published. We will leave these aside and mention only several important English versions that emerged in the 1900s.

James Moffatt, a Scottish scholar, translated the NT into modern English in 1913 and the OT in 1924. The entire Bible, published in 1928, was called *A New Translation of the Bible.* Moffatt was one of the pioneers of modern speech versions.

At the University of Chicago, Edgar J. Goodspeed did something similar to Moffatt's work. His NT, *An American Translation,* was published in 1923; other scholars translated the OT (1927), and the entire Bible appeared in 1931.

English-speaking Roman Catholics had been reading the Douai-Rheims version, published in the sixteenth century and revised by Richard Challoner in the eighteenth. It was based on the Latin Vulgate, as was Ronald Knox's modern speech version of the NT (1945) and the OT (1949). By the time Knox's version appeared,

Catholic scholars had received permission to translate from the original Hebrew and Greek. That led to major translation projects, such as *The Jerusalem Bible* and the *New American Bible*.

During World War II, an Anglican priest, J. B. Phillips, felt the need to put the Scriptures into more understandable English for young people. What came to be *The New Testament in Modern English* was published in stages between 1947 and 1958. It became so popular that he revised it some twenty years later.

During the years that Phillips worked on his translation, a major project got under way in America. About thirty-two scholars, representing most of the major denominations, produced what is called the Revised Standard Version (RSV) of the NT in 1946 and of the whole Bible in 1952.

Although the RSV was subjected to severe criticism, it became so popular that an updated printing was released in 1962, and a second edition in 1971. Since then, it has been thoroughly revised and published in 1989 as the New Revised Standard Version.

Whereas the RSV stands in the tradition of the King James Version of 1611, British scholars, on behalf of most of England's denominations, published *The New English Bible* in 1970 (NT available in 1961). This was a fresh translation of the Hebrew and Greek original texts into modern (British) English. It too has been revised and was published in 1989 as the *Revised English Bible*.

In 1966 the American Bible Society published a modern speech version of the NT, *Good News for Modern Man*. Its popularity led to several revisions, and by 1976 the entire Bible was available as *Good News Bible: Today's English Version*. The translators worked on the principle of "dynamic equivalency," trying to convey in current English the essence of the Hebrew and Greek texts.

In the early 1950s, some evangelical scholars were not happy with the Revised Standard Version and no longer content with the King James Version. They decided to launch a Bible translation project. At least a hundred evangelical scholars from English-speaking countries participated in producing the *Holy Bible: New International Version*, published in 1978 (NT in 1973) and recently revised.

This multitude of English translations (no end is in sight) can be a problem for the modern Bible reader. Moreover, every translation is also an interpretation of the original text. Hence, a survey of some of the major versions does belong to the field of hermeneutics.

Students of the Scriptures frequently ask, Why so many translations? Which translation is more accurate?

First, not all translators follow precisely the same Hebrew or Greek texts. Because the biblical manuscripts do not agree in all their details, translators have to decide which readings to follow. Nevertheless, the many variant readings in our manuscripts do not put in question any major teaching of the Bible.

Second, we must take account of the character of the biblical languages. They have sentence structures different from English. There is then no such thing as a literal translation. There are rarely exact equivalents in English for the Hebrew and Greek words. When words have more than one meaning, the context must guide the translator. Numerous idiomatic expressions in the original text are culturally determined; translators have to recast them so readers will understand their meaning.

Third, like all living languages, English is constantly changing. Many words perfectly clear to readers of the King James Version in 1611 are no longer in common use or their meanings have actually changed.

Fourth, there are different ways of translating. Every

translator or translation team begins by laying down certain translation principles. Some versions move on a relatively high literary level; others use simple language. Some translations are excellent for reading aloud in worship services; others are good study Bibles.

Some Bible translators assume that the readers are familiar with biblical terminology; other translators have a missionary purpose and seek to make the gospel plain to people outside the church. It also makes a big difference whether the translator is revising an existing version or preparing a fresh translation from Hebrew and Greek. Moreover, the translator must decide between sticking rather closely to the original wording or rendering the text more as a paraphrase.

These and other aspects of translation explain the diversity in our English Bibles. Careful Bible students will use several versions so they don't put too much weight on one translation.

5

Biblical Words and Sentences

*T*he books of the OT and NT were produced by prophets and apostles who were inspired by the Holy Spirit (2 Pet. 1:20-21). The inspiration of the Holy Spirit, however, did not do away with the personalities of the individual writers. The Bible books reflect each writer's style and vocabulary.

To understand the messages recorded by the authors of the biblical books, we have to understand the words they use. Communicating by language, whether in writing or orally, cannot be done without words. However, the use of single words still puts severe limits on communication; words need to be put together in a meaningful way. Interpretation, therefore, calls for the correct understanding of biblical words, as well as the phrases, clauses, and sentences in which they are found.

The Meaning of Words

In biblical interpretation we must pay greater attention to words that have profound theological meaning than to those of lesser significance. It profits little to go to the trouble of counting how many times the conjunction *and* appears in the Bible.

Our English versions, as a rule, omit a great many of

the "ands" in the Hebrew. A paratactic language such as Hebrew uses an overabundance of "ands" to string things together. Thus, "and" appears 35 times in Genesis 1. By contrast, if we seek to establish the meanings of words such as *peace, grace, redemption,* or *repentance*, we will be richly rewarded.

Theology, someone has said, is largely philology, in the original sense of that word: "the love of words." Nathan Söderblom of Sweden once put it strikingly: "Philology is the eye of the needle through which the theological camel enters the kingdom of heaven."

We also need to understand the words of the English Bible. Yet it is much more significant to investigate the meanings of the Hebrew and Greek words that lie behind the English.

Few readers of the English Bible can work with the original languages of the Scriptures. Hence, they need to provide themselves with literary tools that open up the meanings of pertinent Hebrew and Greek words. For help in the study of words, we can use biblical lexica and Bible dictionaries with a theological orientation. We do not expect a Webster's dictionary to fill out the biblical meanings of words.

Behind many of the Greek words of the NT stand the Hebrew words of the OT. It is, therefore, not sufficient to look up the meaning of NT words in a classical Greek dictionary, because many of the key words of the NT are informed by their Hebraic background.

The Greek word *peace* (*eirēnē*) may mean simply the absence of strife or war. But when Paul, for example, wishes his readers "peace," he thinks in terms of the Hebrew *shalom*. This Hebrew word has a much fuller meaning, including health, wholeness, fullness of life, and even salvation.

In Greek the verb *to know* (*ginoskō*) may seem merely

intellectual. But behind it lies a Hebrew word (*yada'*) that is much wider and more personal. It is used, for example, of conjugal relations: "The man knew his wife Eve, and she conceived and bore Cain" (Gen. 4:1). Isaiah says the Suffering Servant "knew infirmity" (Isa. 53:3, Hebrew), meaning that he experienced it.

This broader meaning for *know* helps us to understand better some NT texts, such as the following: "This is eternal life, that they may know you, the only true God, and Jesus Christ whom you have sent" (John 17:3). To know means much more than to have information about God or Christ; it means to be personally related to him.

To know the truth means being saved. God desires all people "to be saved and to come to the knowledge of the truth" (1 Tim. 2:4). By taking the Hebraic usage of the verb *know* into account, the NT concept of knowing takes on new dimensions.

Sometimes the etymology of the Hebrew or Greek word helps us understand its basic meaning. Jesus spoke of the coming Holy Spirit as the *paraklētos* (English: *paraclete*, John 14:26). A look at the parts of that word can instruct us. *Para* (cf. English: *parallel*) means "alongside," and *klētos* means "one [who is] called."

Therefore, we may call the Holy Spirit to our side to comfort, help, admonish, warn, teach, encourage, defend, intercede, or plead our cause. A translator will have to ask which of these meanings fits the context of a particular use of *paraklētos*. In 1 John 2:1, *paraklētos* points to the role of Jesus Christ as an "advocate" for sinful believers before the Father, in God's court.

The context is crucial for helping us understand a word's meaning in a particular use. Thus, the English word *love* can have various meanings, such as "intense affection," "sexual desire," "fondness," or "zero score in tennis." Words can be just as ambiguous as symbols. For example, an old wagon wheel, leaning against a wall, can be a snapshot of a ghost town, a restaurant serving country food, a blacksmith shop, a ranch house, or an antique shop. Context means everything in understanding symbols, and words are symbols.

The Septuagint (Greek version of Hebrew OT), for example, translates the Hebrew word *chesed* (steadfast love, covenant loyalty, etc.) in thirteen different ways, depending on the context.

The word *spirit* (Greek: *pneuma*), appearing in 1 Corinthians, is used in different ways. Paul's proclamation was a "demonstration of the Spirit and of power" (2:4); here he clearly means the Holy Spirit. In 2:11 Paul speaks of the "human spirit that is within," and he obviously does not mean the Holy Spirit. We see a third meaning for *spirit* in 2:12; Paul says that the believers have not received "the spirit of the world." A fourth meaning is in 4:21, where Paul asks, whether he shall come with a stick or with a "spirit of gentleness."

In 1 Corinthians 5:5, the backslider's "flesh" is no longer protected from Satan's destructive power, "so that his spirit may be saved in the day of the Lord." "His spirit" stands for the whole new person given to a believer by God's Spirit. Clearly the word *spirit* has a different meaning in each of these passages.

A similar variety of meanings appears with the word *flesh* (Greek: *sarx*), as shown by a few passages in Galatians. "I did not confer with flesh and blood" (1:16, RSV), meaning a "human being." Paul says, "The life I now live in the flesh I live by faith in the Son of God" (2:20). Here the word *flesh* means "body."

In Galatians 5:17, the word *flesh* has a negative meaning and stands for the evil power that orients people against God's reign: "What the Spirit desires is opposed to the flesh." That is also true for the "works of the flesh" (5:19).

According to Galatians 6:13, the Judaizers want to boast about the flesh of the Galatians. Here *flesh* likely refers to circumcision. These few passages, however, do not exhaust all the meanings of the word *flesh*.

Just as the word *flesh* can have both a neutral and a negative meaning, so can the word *world* (Greek: *kosmos*). It is used both for the divinely constituted order of creation as well as the evil system that dominates the lives of sinful human beings. But there are other shades of meaning as well.

Jesus prays that God might glorify him with the glory he had "before the world existed" (John 17:5). That refers to God's creation of the universe. But in John 3:16, where Jesus says, "God so loved the world," he is referring to humanity.

When Paul says, "We brought nothing into the world," he means life as lived here on this earth (1 Tim. 6:7).

A negative meaning of the word *world* is found in 1 John 2:15-17. There believers are told not to love this world, for here "world" is described as "the desire of the flesh, the desire of the eyes, the pride in riches." As in James 1:27, this means all that is alienated from God.

Besides etymology and context, it is important to know something of the history of words. The word for *church* (*ekklēsia*) is sometimes understood simply in terms of its etymology—*ek*, meaning "out"; and *kaleō*, meaning "to call." Some people then build on such an understanding of *ekklēsia* to stress the church being "called out" and separate from the rest of society. But we should not put the weight of the meaning of *ekklēsia* on being called out.

In ancient Greece, *ekklēsia* was a well-known word

for a city's assembly of citizens. It did not start as a religious word. However, when the OT was translated into Greek, *ekklēsia* was chosen to translate the Hebrew *qahal*, used for the assembly of the people of God, Israel. When the NT was written, the word *ekklēsia*, with its dual background, secular and religious, became a useful word to designate the assemblies of God's new people, the Christian churches, or the church as a whole.

The NT writers had another Greek word available with a similar meaning, *sunagōgē*, which also means a "gathering" or "assembly." James (2:2) uses it for a Christian assembly. In time, it came to be reserved for Jewish assemblies, and the gathering of Christians was called an *ekklēsia*.

Another example of a word with an important history is *parousia* (coming, presence, arrival). The etymology of the word (*para* with the verb "to be," meaning "to be present") does not give us the complete picture. It, too, was a nonreligious word in its early usage, referring to the arrival and visit of royalty. Secular papyri, for example, speak of the emperor's *parousia* when he visits a city.

The NT writers chose this word *parousia* to designate, among other things, the coming of Jesus at the end of this age (as in 1 Thess. 4:15). It is another illustration of how a well-known word, with certain connotations in first-century society, was chosen by the biblical writers, "baptized into Christ," as it were, and used for theological purposes.

A century ago the meanings of some NT Greek words were not yet known, because they were not otherwise found in ancient Greek literature. However, with the discovery of secular papyri written in the common Greek of the NT and further study of Greek authors, many words are better understood. Readers may have wondered, in the parable of the prodigal son, how the younger son could have gathered everything together (clothes, cattle, land?) and gone off into the far country.

The word *sunagō* literally means "to gather together" (Luke 15:13), and most English versions still render it that way. The *New English Bible*, however, says that the son turned everything into cash and left home. The verb *sunagō* could have that meaning in the first century (as in Plutarch).

Many English words in the Bible are derived from Greek words. However, we can make serious mistakes if we read the meanings of these English derivatives back into the original Greek words. For example, the Greek word for witness is *martus*, from which comes the English word *martyr*. But it is a mistake to read *martyr* into every occurrence of the word *martus* in the Bible. The original meaning is "witness," and only later, after many Christian witnesses had died for their faith, did this word take on the meaning of "martyr."

It is true that our word *dynamite* is derived from the Greek word for "power" (*dunamis*). But the concept of "power" predates by many centuries Alfred Nobel's discovery of dynamite (1866). So we must not read the English word *dynamite* back into the Greek word for "power."

The etymology, the usage, the history of a word, and the context in which it stands in the Scriptures—these are different aspects of word study.

It is also important to observe that simple words, whose meanings seem to be perfectly clear, do not always have the same range of meaning that we might expect. The word *all* or *every* is an example. Mark tells us that the "whole Judean country and all the people of Jerusalem were going out to [John] and were baptized in the river Jordan" (1:5). But we know that not everyone was baptized. In fact, Luke tells us that the Pharisees and the lawyers refused to be baptized (7:30).

Mark says that Jesus "cured many" (1:34), and Matthew says he "cured all who were sick" (8:16). In Hebrew, *all* and *many* are sometimes used interchangeably. Similarly, when Jesus said that he had come to give his life as a ransom "for many" (Mark 10:45), or that his blood was poured out "for many" (Mark 14:24), he meant "all" (cf. Isa. 53:11-12).

If we are to read the biblical text correctly, word study is important. Nevertheless, words are connected with other words to form phrases, clauses, and sentences. Sentence structure must also be carefully studied, if we are to capture the gist of what the biblical writers want to say to us.

Sentence Structure

Grammar, said Martin Luther, is the maidservant of theology. Since the Bible is literature, no one reading the Bible can afford to think lightly of grammar. Although the grammar of the English Bible must also be taken seriously, translators and interpreters are particularly interested in the Hebrew and Greek grammar behind the translations.

When we speak of grammar, we mean words and their various forms (morphology), and the grouping of words into larger units (syntax). Since Hebrew and Greek belong to different families of languages, their sentence structures are quite different.

Hebrew is paratactic in structure, with principal clauses connected by conjunctions. Greek is hypotactic: principal clauses are often followed by a number of subordinate clauses. This is not the place to describe in detail the grammar of Hebrew or Greek. A few illustrations may underscore the importance of grammar in determining the correct meaning of sentences.

It is important that conjunctions, such as *and, but, therefore, because, since, in order, so that, before,* and others be carefully observed.

For example, in Mark 4:12, Jesus seems to suggest that he uses parables "in order that" (Greek: *hina*) people may not understand his message and be converted. But surely Jesus did not use parables expressly for the purpose of covering up the truth and hardening people's hearts!

In Jewish thought, purpose and result were often not distinguished. Mark 4:12 may be speaking chiefly of result. According to parallel texts, the people's refusal to believe brings spiritual blindness upon themselves, which is confirmed when Jesus begins to speak in parables (cf. Isa. 6:9-10; Matt. 13:15; Luke 8:10; John 12:39-41; Acts 28:26-27; on this further, see chap. 11, below, under heading "Why Did Jesus Use Parables?").

Prepositions are also extremely important. In Galatians 4:13, Paul states that he came to Galatia with the gospel "on account of" or "because of" physical infirmity (*dia* with the accusative). Older English versions usually give it as "through" infirmity, but that changes the meaning of the preposition.

The same Greek preposition *dia* (now with the genitive) is found in 1 Timothy 2:15: the woman "will be saved *through* childbearing." Surely Paul is not saying that the bearing of children is a means for women to obtain salvation! *Dia* must have a different sense here.

Although the tense, voice, or mood of verbs may not be directly related to sentence structure, they certainly play a significant role in the interpretation of the biblical text. When Paul exhorts his readers to be filled with the Spirit (Eph. 5:18), the verb is in the imperative mood, in the passive voice, and also in the present tense. The implication is that this is not a once-for-all experience. The filling can and should be repeated; it is an ongoing experience, and God does the filling.

When the apostle John (1 John 3:9) claims that those who are born of God do not sin, the present tense of the verb "sin" is important. In Greek, the present tense normally implies ongoing action. Hence, we may say that a true believer does not continue to sin and does not live in sin. Moreover, the apostle has already told readers that "if we say that we have no sin, we deceive ourselves" (1:8). Believers who sin have an advocate with the Father (2:1).

It is interesting to observe the different tenses of the word *to save* and the timing of salvation. In Titus 3:5, the apostle states that God has saved us through the coming of Jesus—a past event. In Ephesians 2:8, we also have a past tense, but the verb "saved" is in the perfect tense: "By grace you have been saved," and now we are saved.

In 1 Corinthians 1:18, however, the tense of the verb is present: "To us who are being saved," the word of the cross is God's power. Salvation, then, is something also ongoing in the present.

When we turn to Romans 5:10, however, salvation lies in the future: "We will be saved by his life." It is a salvation also to be revealed on the last day (1 Pet. 1:5). That helps to expand our understanding of salvation.

We need to take into account many other grammatical details when we grapple with the meaning of the biblical text. Verbs and nouns, adverbs and adjectives, pronouns and prepositions—all must be carefully observed. Above all we must focus on clauses, sentences, and entire paragraphs, if we want to catch the full import of what the writer is saying.

6

Figurative Speech

Some Bible readers are unsettled by the whole idea of finding biblical figures of speech, such as metaphors or similes. The Bible has to be interpreted literally, they say. If we suggest that the biblical writers used figurative language, we do not take the message of the Scriptures seriously, they claim.

One devout Bible reader insisted that when Paul, in his letter to the Corinthians, warns his readers not to build with "wood, hay, straw" (1 Cor. 3:12), he meant wood, hay, and straw. True, but we must then ask, What was the apostle's purpose? Surely he wasn't advising the Corinthians on materials for building their houses!

Instead, Paul was warning them not to engage in the work of God's kingdom in such a way that their work would not pass God's scrutiny in the final judgment. Wood, hay and stubble are figures of speech for combustible material, in contrast to gold, silver, and precious stones that can stand the test of fire.

Failure to observe figurative language has led to tragic consequences in the history of the church. The great Alexandrian teacher Origen took Jesus' saying literally about cutting off the hand if it causes sin. He applied it to his sexual desires and took the radical step of having himself emasculated.

A woman sought guidance from the Word of God

about her troubled marriage. The counselor encouraged her to divorce her husband and marry another man, because Paul exhorted readers to "put on the new man" (Eph. 4:24, KJV).

A female college student took Paul's advice "Lay hands suddenly on no man" (1 Tim. 5:22, KJV) to mean "Don't rush into marriage." This was a good guideline but based on interpretation that missed Paul's intent.

When figurative language is treated as literal, the application of Scripture may seem amusing. Some sixteenth-century Anabaptists preached from rooftops. After all, Jesus had said, "What you hear whispered, proclaim from the housetops" (Matt. 10:27).

Certain modern English versions have tried to avoid figures of speech. Readers must have some degree of appreciation for literature in general to understand them. The *Good News Bible* was published especially for readers whose first language may not be English. Hence, figures of speech are kept to a minimum. When Paul mentions several apostles as "pillars" in the church (Gal. 2:9), GNB has "who seemed to be the leaders."

Instead of saying that Pilate had "mingled" the blood of the worshipers "with their sacrifices" (Luke 13:1), the GNB says "Pilate had killed [them] while they were offering sacrifices to God." Paul speaks of having an "open door" in Ephesus (1 Cor. 16:9); GNB: "There is a real opportunity here."

It takes a little sophistication to capture the import of figures of speech. Young children, whose facility in the use of language is still limited, are sometimes baffled by our use of figurative language. German professor Helmut Thielicke writes that as a young child at home, he dreaded going to kindergarten. A *Kindergarten* (German: garden for children), he imagined, was a garden where children were planted in the ground and watered to make them grow.

The picture-language of the Bible was in part determined by its surrounding culture. When Isaiah says, "Though your sins are like scarlet, they shall be as white as snow" (1:18), he assumes that his hearers know about snow. Otherwise his comparison would not have made sense. In desert regions where snow is not known, attempts have been made to replace *snow* with words such as "white sand," to convey the right message.

Those not familiar with ancient farming methods find it hard to understand what Christ said to Paul when he confronted him on the way to Damascus: "It hurts you to kick against the goads"(Acts 26:14).

The picture-language of the Bible is rich and diverse. We must try to classify figures of speech and illustrate how they are used.

Comparisons

Indirect Comparisons. Such comparisons are called *similes.* In English, words such as *like* or *as* indicate the comparison. The daughter of Zion, says Isaiah, is "left like a booth in a vineyard, like a shelter in a cucumber field, like a besieged city" (1:8). Here we see three comparisons in one verse.

Hosea is particularly good at making comparisons. Israel is compared to "stubborn heifer" (4:16). Israel's love for God is like a "morning cloud, like the dew that goes away early" (6:4). Israel has become like "a defective bow" (7:16). Interpreters must seek to uncover the meaning of such figures of speech.

In the NT, Jesus says, "See, I am sending you out like lambs into the midst of wolves" (Luke 10:3). "Be wise as serpents and innocent as doves" (Matt. 10:16). "For as the lightning comes from the east and flashes as far as the west, so will be the coming for the Son of Man" (24:27).

Paul writes, "The day of the Lord will come like a thief in the night" (1 Thess. 5:2). "Then sudden destruction will come upon them, as labor pains come upon a pregnant woman, and there will be no escape" (1 Thess. 5:3). Peter says that the devil prowls around "like a roaring lion, . . . looking for someone to devour" (1 Pet. 5:8).

Interpreters have the task of identifying the point of the comparison. For example, the psalmist likens the loving relationship of family members to "the precious oil on the head, running down upon . . . the beard of Aaron" (Ps. 133:1-2). He probably had the pleasant fragrance of the oil in mind. Surely he did not have the oiliness of the ointment or the attractiveness of Aaron's beard in mind. Moreover, this simile cannot be understood at all if readers have no familiarity with Israel's religious practices.

These are a few illustrations of how indirect comparisons enliven communication.

Direct Comparisons. Direct comparisons are called *metaphors.* Metaphors are often temporally and culturally determined. This sometimes makes it difficult for later generations to understand their meaning. Will the next generation, not knowing Margaret Thatcher, understand who is meant when someone mentions "the iron lady"?

The prophet Isaiah cries out, "All people are grass" (40:6); this is a direct comparison. He goes on to say, "Their constancy is like the flower of the field"; this is a simile. Using metaphors, God promises Jeremiah that he has made him "a fortified city, an iron pillar, and a bronze wall, against the whole land" (Jer. 1:18).

Hosea says that Israel is "a cake not turned" (7:8): the nation has prospered economically and made progress culturally (well baked on that side), but spiritually and morally Israel is "unbaked" and inedible. The psalmist writes, "The voice of the Lord flashes forth flames of fire" (29:7).

John the Baptist calls the Pharisees and Sadducees, who rejected the message of the inbreaking of God's kingdom, "a brood of vipers" (Matt. 3:7). Jesus also frequently makes use of metaphors. He calls his disciples "the salt of the earth" and "the light of the world" (Matt. 5:13-14). They are the "little flock" (Luke 12:32). Herod is a "fox" (Luke 13:32); Jesus did not mean Herod is furry or has four legs, but that he is crafty and cunning.

It is not possible to understand the NT concept of the church if we overlook the numerous metaphors used to portray it. The church is Christ's body, a temple, a family, a royal priesthood, twelve tribes, the chosen race, Abraham's children, the new creation, the bride of Christ, and so on. Bible readers should be careful not to construct their theology of the church on a single metaphor.

The apostle Paul stands out in his use of metaphors. He draws on imagery taken, for example, from the realm of agriculture. To the Corinthians, he writes, "I planted, Apollos watered, but God gave the growth" (1 Cor. 3:6). God's servants are farmers who "have the first share of the crops" (2 Tim. 2:6). He also uses metaphors from the military: "The weapons of our warfare are not merely human . . . to destroy strongholds" (2 Cor. 10:4). The Christian's armor in his battle against evil is described in great detail in Ephesians 6:10-17.

Some of Paul's figures of speech are taken from the realm of architecture. He says he is "like a skilled master builder" (1 Cor. 3:10; simile), who laid the foundation of the church in Corinth. When believers die, they hope for "a house not made with hands, eternal in the heavens" (2 Cor. 5:1; metaphor), in contrast to the "tent" in which they now live. The church is called a building that "grows into a holy temple in the Lord" (Eph. 2:21).

Paul also makes use of figures of speech from the sports world. He is a runner who does not run aimlessly, a boxer who does not beat the air (1 Cor. 9:26). "I press on toward the goal for the prize of the heavenly call of God in Christ Jesus" (Phil. 3:14). He chides the Galatian readers, "You were running well; who prevented you from obeying the truth?" (Gal. 5:7).

Then there are metaphors from the courtroom. The well-known doctrine of justification by faith is expressed in legal terms. Paul also speaks of appearing before the judgment seat of Christ (2 Cor. 5:10). He tells his Corinthian critics that it is a small thing for him to be judged by them "or by any human court" (1 Cor. 4:3). Paul calls the church to "judge" "those who are inside" (5:12). Besides legal terms, Paul also speaks of the heavenly "citizenship" of believers (Phil. 3:20).

The apostle also uses metaphors derived from the social life of his day. Repeatedly he calls himself and other servants of Christ "slaves" (*douloi*) . He is using the language of release from slavery when he says redemption was a purchase: "you were bought with a price" (1 Cor. 6:20).

The nautical world also provides Paul with figures of speech. He knows of people who have suffered shipwreck in their faith (1 Tim. 1:19). The gift of leadership is called *kubērnēsis* (1 Cor. 12:28); a captain of a ship, the helmsman, was the *kubernētēs*. There is also the whole realm of the Jewish temple ritual that offers many figures of speech.

When the biblical writers speak of God, they frequently use metaphorical language. God is Father, Deliverer, Warrior, Husband, and so forth. References to God's hand, his eye, his arm, his feet, and his mouth are called *anthropomorphisms*, speaking of God as though in human form. They belong to the realm of metaphor. We also have *anthropopathisms*, describing God's feelings in human terms: anger, repentance, sorrow, and jealousy.

Christ is described as King, Lord, Lamb of God, root of David, bright morning star, and the like.

Direct and indirect comparisons require readers to have some knowledge of the culture in which they were readily understood. Yet some figures of speech elude us because we no longer know their original significance.

One such case might be Romans 12:20, where Paul cautions against taking revenge against those who do us wrong. If we do them good, we will "heap burning coals on their heads." That's a quotation from Proverbs 25:22. But what does it mean? It sounds more like vengeance than forgiveness, but the context does not allow that.

Some interpreters think it means that if we do our enemies good, it will put them to shame (so that their heads "burn"). Recently an Egyptian ritual was discovered: When an evildoer is sorry for what he has done, he comes with fiery coals in a container on his head to meet the person he victimized. This is a sign that he is seeking reconciliation. With the coals, he is likely prepared to cook a meal celebrating renewed friendship.

This ritual fits a social setting where cooking fires were maintained. Anyone who let such a fire go out would be in trouble. A neighbor might supply live coals to start the fire. Insulated in ashes, the coals were carried in a brazier on the head. Thus it was a good deed to share coals of fire.

Beyond direct and indirect comparisons, there are other figures of speech important for Bible study.

Metonymy

In this figure of speech, something is named by substituting one of its attributes or an associated term for the thing itself. For example, when we say that the White House has announced something, we assume it is from the president of the United States. If the Vatican makes a declaration, we think of the pope as the source.

All over the world, Christians regularly pray, "Give us this day our daily bread." Yet their staple food may not be bread but perhaps rice or potatoes. Bread, by metonymy, stands for daily sustenance, for food.

The prophet Isaiah promises Eliakim the key to the house of David (22:22). Of course, neither the word "key" nor the word "house" are to be understood in the literal sense. He means that he will have authority over David's descendants.

In the parable of the rich man and Lazarus, Abraham tells the rich man in Hades that his brothers have "Moses and the prophets." Abraham knows that both Moses and the prophets were long gone. What he meant was that they had Scriptures from Moses and the prophets (Luke 16:29; cf. 24:44). Matthew says "Jerusalem, and all Judea, and all the region round about Jordan" went out to hear John the Baptist (3:5, KJV). He means the people living in Jerusalem, in Judea, and in all the region round about Jordan. Because the name of God was considered to be so holy in Israel, they often used substitutes for the name of God. When the prodigal son returns home, he confesses, "Father, I have sinned against heaven and before you" (Luke 15:21). *Heaven* means *God*. For that reason, it is also wrong to distinguish between "kingdom of God" and "kingdom of heaven," as in the Gospels.

Sometimes when a word is used as a substitute for something else, we are at a loss to know precisely what is meant. In 1 Thessalonians 4:4, Paul says each reader should keep "his vessel" (KJV) in "holiness and honor" (NRSV). What does he mean by "vessel"? Some versions interpret this word as "body," and others as "wife." Both are possible. Our bodies are called "earthen vessels" (2 Cor. 4:7, KJV), and the wife is called the "weaker vessel" (1 Pet. 3:7, KJV). Paul is said to be Christ's "chosen vessel" (Acts 9:15, KJV), God's agent to bring the gospel to the Gentiles.

In a case like this, only the context can guide us, but the context of 1 Thessalonians 4:4 does not allow us to be dogmatic. It looks as if Paul is speaking of winning a wife in holiness and honor. But it could also mean that believers are to learn to control their bodily urges.

The Lord of the church advises Laodicea to purchase white clothes (Rev. 3:18). Clothes stand for a person's character and manner of life. The redeemed who come home to glory "have washed their robes and made them white in the blood of the Lamb" (Rev. 7:14). Robes represent a person's character (cf. 19:8), and "blood" stands for Christ's sacrificial death.

Personification

When biblical authors speak of inanimate things as they would speak of people, we have personification. Thunder speaks, waters rejoice, hills clap their hands, and nature puts on clothes of mourning. Such personification makes communication vivid.

The OT is full of examples of personification. Here are a few illustrations from the NT. The Scriptures speak (John 7:38); the word of God runs (2 Thess. 3:1, from Greek); God's word is living (Heb. 4:12). At the cross, Christ killed the enmity between Jews and Gentiles (Eph. 2:16, KJV). "Enmity" is portrayed as a person. Sin also is personified: "For sin, seizing an opportunity in the commandment, deceived me and through it killed me" (Rom. 7:11). Love is personified in 1 Corinthians 13: fifteen verbs tell us what love does or does not do.

In the last book of the Bible, Hades is personified as following Death, the rider of the pale green horse (Rev. 6:8). In the end, Death and Hades are cast into the lake of fire (20:14). When this present age comes to an end, the ungodly call on the rocks and the mountains to fall upon them and protect them from the wrath of the Lamb (6:16). The rocks and the mountains are treated as if they were persons. The beast is given a mouth to utter haughty and blasphemous words (13:5). The beast is personified, given human attributes.

Euphemisms

In every human society, there are subjects about which we do not speak openly. Instead, we use idioms that are called euphemisms (Greek: *eu*, good; *phēmi*, to speak). These are milder or more roundabout ways of mentioning what may otherwise be embarrassing, offensive, or distasteful.

Instead of saying that Adam and Eve had sexual intercourse, the narrator says that "the man knew his wife" (Gen. 4:1). "To touch a woman" (1 Cor. 7:1) or "lie with" one of the opposite sex (Gen. 19:32) is also a euphemism for sexual intercourse.

When Laban catches up with Jacob, who has fled with his family and flocks, he wants to know who has stolen his household gods. Rachel has put them into the camel's saddle and is sitting on them. When her father begins searching for them, she says she can't get up "for the way of women is upon me" (Gen. 31:35), meaning that she is having her menstrual period.

When the servants of Ehud cannot find their master, they surmise that he "covereth his feet" (Judg. 3:24, KJV), is relieving himself. "Covering one's feet" is a euphemism for what we euphemistically describe as "going to the bathroom." The "hair of the feet" (Isa. 7:20) that the king of Assyria will shave means pubic hair; feet is a euphemism for the genitals (Exod. 4:25).

How openly we speak of sexual activity or of other bodily functions depends on our culture. Certain things may be taboo in one society but not in another.

Most societies view death as an enemy and often use euphemisms when speaking of death. Death may be described as the plucking up of the tent-cord (Job 4:21; cf. 2 Cor. 5:1-2), the removal of your dwelling (Isa. 38:12), being sent to the land of silence (Ps. 94:17), or going to your ancestors (Gen. 15:15).

In Judaism, a common euphemism for death was sleep (1 Kings 2:10). When Jesus says Lazarus is sleeping, the disciples take that word literally until Jesus explains that Lazarus is dead (John 11:11-14). Paul writes to the Corinthians, "We shall not all sleep, but we shall all be changed" (1 Cor. 15:51, KJV). He tells the Thessalonians that he does not want the brothers and sisters to be "ignorant" concerning "those who are asleep" (1 Thess. 4:13-14, RSV), "those who have died" (NRSV).

Idolatry was another area of life in which Judaism came to use euphemisms. After the exile, names of pagan deities became so distasteful that readers in the synagogue substituted the word *bosheth* (shame) for Baal, Astarte, Molech, and others. The name Mephibosheth is an intentional corruption of Meribbaal (cf. 2 Sam. 4:4; 1 Chron. 8:34), and Ish-bosheth, "man of shame," replaces Ishbaal (2 Sam. 2:8).

Translators sometimes introduce euphemisms where the Hebrew and Greek Scriptures do not have them. In some instances, what was inoffensive in biblical times can be embarrassing in a different culture. Paul, for example, commends the Galatians for receiving him so kindly, in spite of his physical condition; they did not "spit out" and thereby despise him. Most translators avoid a literal translation, even though they can hear the spitting sound in the Greek verb *ekptuō* (Gal. 4:14).

Hyperbole

When people exaggerate or overstate something to stress or underscore what they are saying, we call that hyperbole. It has nothing to do with deception; they do not mean for others to take the hyperbolic expressions literally. The Bible also makes use of hyperbolic language. Some Christians find that hard to accept. For them, exaggeration means imprecision or even falsehood. But as long as both writer and reader understand this literary form, hyperbole is a useful way of expressing feelings or emotions.

For example, we read that Saul and Jonathan were "swifter than eagles, . . . stronger than lions" (2 Sam. 1:23). Such comparisons must be taken with the proverbial grain of salt.

God promises Abraham that his descendants will be like the dust of the earth (Gen. 13:16), the stars of heaven (15:5), or the sand of the seashore (22:17). None of these can be counted.

Before the Israelite conquest, their spies report that the inhabitants of Canaan have cities so high that they reach into heaven (Deut. 1:28). The camels of the Midianites, Israel's enemies, are like sand on the seashore in number, we are told (Judg. 7:12).

The psalmist describes his sorrow in graphic fashion: "Every night I flood my bed with tears; I drench my couch with weeping" (6:6).

Mark 1:5 reports that all of Judea and Jerusalem went out to be baptized by John, but he surely means "many" rather than "all" in its absolute sense. Jesus tells his disciples that if they have faith like a mustard seed, they will be able to say to the mountain, "Move from here to there," and it will move (Matt. 17:20). Rarely does a Bible reader expect literally to remove mountains by faith. This is figurative language, and it is also hyperbolic.

John the apostle says that if all the things Jesus did were recorded, the world would not be able to contain the books that would be written (John 21:25). The enemies of Jesus are forced to acknowledge, that "the world" is going after Jesus (John 12:19). Luke writes that the Athenians spend all their time telling or hearing something new (Acts 17:20). Members of the synagogue in Thessalonica accuse Paul and Silas of "turning the world upside down" (Acts 17:6).

We need to have a sense of humor to fully appreciate hyperbole. Jesus repeatedly makes use of hyperbole to underscore some truth. He compares the speck in your neighbor's eye to the log in your own eye (Matt. 7:3).

Jesus warns that it is easier for a camel to get through the eye of a needle than for a rich man to get into the kingdom of God (Mark 10:25). Because this statement is so hyperbolic, various attempts have been made to water it down. Some claim that Jesus meant a small city gate, but there is no evidence for that line of interpretation. Others have read *kamilos* (rope, cable, hawser) instead of *kamelos* (camel), but that is not the correct reading of the text. The imagery is deliberately grotesque.

When the apostle John describes the final battle between God and the forces of evil, he uses hyperbolic language: the blood of the slain will be up to the bridles of the horses (Rev. 14:20). Josephus uses almost identical language in describing the destruction of Jerusalem. We don't have to ask whether such phenomena are physically possible.

Litotes

When an assertion is made in which the opposite is negated, we call that a litotes. Thus Jesus told his disciples, "You shall be baptized with the Holy Spirit not many days from now" (Acts 1:5); he meant in a few days from now. Luke reports that there was no small commotion among the soldiers guarding Peter when they discovered in the morning that he was gone (Acts 12:18); in other words, there was a great commotion.

The silversmith Demetrius brought "no little business to the artisans" (Acts 19:24), meaning much business. On Paul's sea voyage to Rome, "no small tempest raged," endangering the lives of the travelers and causing a shipwreck (Acts 27:20, 41).

Irony

Irony is used in discourse when people in a playful manner say the opposite of what they actually mean. Job tells his friends that wisdom will die with them (12:2). It's a sarcastic way of saying that they think they know everything there is to know. David's wife Michal expresses her disdain for her husband: "How the king of Israel honored himself today, uncovering himself today before the eyes of his servants" (2 Sam. 6:20).

Irony can also express incongruity: Jesus says to the scribes and Pharisees, "How beautifull [*kalōs*] Isaiah prophesied about you hypocrites" (Mark 7:6, author's trans.). He accuses them of building tombs for the prophets and decorating the graves of the righteous, when they actually are like their ancestors who murdered the prophets (Matt. 23:29).

Paul likewise points out incongruity in the lives of the Corinthians who were "puffed up" with their own spirituality: "Already you have all you want! Already you have become rich! . . . Indeed, I wish you had

become kings, so that we might be kings with you"
(1 Cor. 4:6-8). He speaks to those who put much stock in
their ability to speak in tongues: "You may give thanks
well enough, but the other person is not built up"
(1 Cor. 14:17), not being able to understand.

Synecdoche

When a part is used for the whole, or the whole for a
part, or an individual for class, we have a figure of
speech called synecdoche (Greek: *sun*, together; *ek*,
from; *dechomai*, take). According to Luke, the emperor
decreed that the whole world should be registered
(Luke 2:1). He obviously means the people of the
Roman world, not including "barbarians" (Rom. 1:14).
The whole is used for a part.

That is also how we should understand the three
days and three nights that Jesus was in the grave (Matt.
12:40). Jesus did not necessarily mean seventy-two
hours. "For three days and three nights" is an alternate
way of saying that he was raised "on the third day." A
part of a day counts as a whole.

The three thousand "souls" converted on the day of
Pentecost and then baptized were "people" (Acts 2:41,
KJV). In Acts 1:15 (KJV) we are told that 120 "names"
were gathered together, meaning "people."

It is almost impossible to converse meaningfully
without using figures of speech. Without them, our conversation would be matter of fact and drab. The
Scriptures also make abundant use of them. Interpreters
need to handle figures of speech as figurative rather
than in a woodenly literal fashion. Only then can we be
fair to the biblical writers and understand what they
meant.

7

The Use of Symbolism

*T*he biblical writers repeatedly describe actions that have symbolical meaning or theological import. Prophets and apostles occasionally received their messages from God in the form of visions or dreams. Occasionally inanimate objects conveyed messages to the recipients of divine revelation and later to readers of the Bible. Even numbers can be used in a symbolical manner, as well as names, colors, and the like.

Symbolism might have been properly treated under the heading of figurative speech, but we have chosen to discuss it under a separate heading.

Symbolical Acts

At the end of Solomon's reign, the prophet Ahijah has clothed himself with a new garment. When he meets Jeroboam, he tears it into twelve pieces and asks Jeroboam to take ten pieces (1 Kings 11:30-31). This action symbolizes that the kingdom will be divided and Jeroboam will rule over ten northern tribes, the kingdom of Israel. Judah (and Benjamin, 12:23) will be left as the Southern Kingdom.

The Lord asks the prophet Jeremiah to buy a loin-cloth and go to the river Euphrates and hide it. When he retrieves it, it is ruined. The meaning of this symbolical act is that the people of Judah, who have become apostate, are like the ruined loincloth, good for nothing (Jer. 13:1-9).

On another occasion, the Lord commands Jeremiah to go to the potter and buy an earthenware jug. He is to smash the jug in the presence of the rulers and inhabitants of Jerusalem. The Lord explains the symbolic action: "So will I break this people and this city, as one breaks a potter's vessel, so that it can never be mended" (Jer. 19:11).

The Lord tells Jeremiah to make a yoke and put it on his neck. This is a warning to leaders of Judah: "Bring your necks under the yoke of the king of Babylon." Do not conspire to revolt (Jer. 27–28).

When the Babylonians are at the gates of Jerusalem, the Lord tells Jeremiah to go to Anathoth and buy a field. The command makes no sense in the face of the disaster about to overtake Jerusalem. But the Lord explains: "For thus says the Lord of hosts, the God of Israel: Houses and fields and vineyards shall again be bought in this land" (32:15). Purchasing a field at that moment was a symbolical act, showing hope for the future.

Ezekiel takes a brick and portrays the city of Jerusalem with siegeworks around it, together with a military camp and battering rams. It is to symbolize the imminent demise of Jerusalem at the hands of the Babylonians (Ezek. 4:1-3). Then the prophet is to lie first on his left side and then on his right for a long time, and eat food that is defiled. "Thus shall the people of Israel eat their bread, unclean, among the nations to which I will drive them" (Ezek. 4:13).

We have symbolical acts in the NT as well. When Jesus sends out his disciples on a mission, he warns them that they will not be received with open arms everywhere. In that case, they should shake the dust from their feet and leave the city (Matt. 10:14).

Every Jew understood this gesture; it meant that such a Jewish town was considered pagan. It was common practice, when Jews returned from Gentile lands, that they would shake the dust off their feet. Paul and Barnabas, in fact, shook the dust from their feet when they left Antioch of Pisidia, where the Jewish authorities opposed their message (Acts 13:51).

In the Gospel of John, the marvelous deeds of Jesus are regularly called "signs." Likely the apostle meant that Jesus' wonderful works pointed beyond themselves to some significant theological truth. When Jesus walks upon the water, that is a miracle. Yet that act signifies also that he is the Lord over all evil powers, for the sea was often seen as an evil power. Jesus' entry into Jerusalem, riding on a donkey, is a messianic act, as is the act of cursing the fig tree, washing the disciples' feet, or the cleansing of the temple.

The high priest Caiaphas tears his clothes when Jesus is arraigned before him (Mark 14:63). That is a symbolical act, suggesting that Jesus has blasphemed. When Pilate washes his hands, he uses a symbolical act to reinforce his claim that he is "innocent of this man's blood" (Matt. 27:24; cf. Ps. 73:13).

The prophet Agabus takes Paul's belt and ties his own hands and feet with it to signify Paul's coming arrest and captivity (Acts 21:11).

Symbolical Visions

The prophet Amos has a vision in which someone makes locusts (7:1-2) that eat the grass of the land. The Lord also shows him a shower of fire that devours the great deep (the sea) and eats up the land (7:4). After that Amos sees the Lord standing beside a wall with a plumb line in his hand (7:7). When the Lord asks Amos what he sees, Amos answers, "A plumb line."

Then comes the interpretation: God is about to judge Israel. The Lord then shows him a basket of summer fruit (*qayits*) and gives him the interpretation: "the end (*qets*) has come upon my people" (8:1-2). Notice the wordplay in Hebrew!

King Nebuchadnezzar has a dream, and Daniel is asked to interpret it for him. In his dream, he sees a statue made of different kinds of metals. But then a stone smashes the image and becomes a great mountain that fills the earth (2:31-35). Daniel explains that the different metals represent successive kingdoms of the world. In the end they are all demolished, and only God's kingdom survives (2:44).

Daniel himself has dreams and visions. First he sees three beasts arise from the sea—a lion, a bear, and a leopard. Then follows a fourth beast that is strong and dreadful in appearance and crushes everything in its path. As the vision unfolds, this beast is destroyed and the other beasts also lose their dominion.

Finally, Daniel sees a figure like a son of man, coming with the clouds of heaven, to whom the Ancient of Days gives a kingdom that shall not pass away (7:1-14, RSV). The meaning is clear: all the kingdoms of this world are temporary and eventually vanish; only the kingdom of God is eternal.

The last book of the Bible is rich in symbolism, typical of apocalyptic literature of the time. John, for example, sees a two-edged sword coming out of the mouth of the exalted Christ (Rev. 1:16). This conveys the message that he is the Lord over life and death, and that he judges with his word (cf. 19:15). The four horsemen John sees riding across the pages of history symbolize the destructive powers of evil that characterize human history (6:1-8).

The meaning of a vision may not be explicit, especially to readers in a different thought world. For example, John sees a heavenly woman about to bear a child, and a dragon stands ready to devour it. This woman, initially at least, seems to symbolize Israel, through whom Messiah comes into the world. But after the child is taken into heaven (Rev. 12:5), the dragon pursues the woman (12:13). In that setting, she seems to represent the new people of God, the church. One symbol can convey more than one truth.

The beast John sees arising from the sea has a mortal wound that has healed (Rev. 13:3). The symbol indicates that anti-Christian powers go down in defeat but continue to rise again. Christian readers should, therefore, not think that with the death of one evil leader, such as Nero, the powers of evil have been defeated. Evil powers rise out of the slimy depths again and again until Christ returns and makes an end of all resistance to God (Rev. 17:11-14).

Repeatedly Revelation says that John "saw." The apostle then portrays for us what he saw. These word pictures must, however, not be understood in the bald literal sense. John reminds us upon occasion that these visions must be understood symbolically, spiritually, and allegorically.

For example, the two witnesses are killed for their testimony, and their bodies lie on the street of the great city called "Sodom and Egypt, where also their Lord was crucified" (11:8). Sodom represents the ultimate in wickedness, and Egypt is the land of Israel's slavery. Both are to be taken symbolically, says John (11:8, GNB).

Material Symbols

When God calls Moses to deliver Israel from slavery in Egypt, he reveals himself to Moses at the burning bush

(Exod. 3:2). Whatever else the burning bush may mean, fire represents God's holy presence.

Repeatedly in the Bible, radiant glory and dazzling clothing symbolize being close to heaven and the presence of God (Exod. 34:35; Luke 9:29; Matt. 28:3; 2 Cor. 3:7-18). This is especially characteristic of visions (Ezek. 1; Dan. 10:5-7; Luke 2:9; Rev. 1:12-16).

The various furnishings and utensils of the tabernacle all symbolize some truth: the altars, the table, the lampstand with its seven lamps, the ark of the covenant, and other items (Exod. 25ff.). However, to read NT truths back into these furnishings and to find hidden meanings in such details as the wood, the silver sockets, and so forth, is not helpful. That does not deny the rich typology of the tabernacle; yet the furnishings also had a symbolical meaning.

Blood is also a material symbol. The word itself can have different connotations, depending on the context in which it is used. Shedding blood can mean murder (Matt. 23:30). We also have redemption "by his blood" (Rev. 1:5), where blood symbolizes Christ's sacrificial death; he gave his life for us. The *Good News Bible* says, "By his death he has freed us from our sins." It uses the word "death" instead of "blood," since blood is a symbol of death. Since, however, Christ's sacrificial death is meant, perhaps the word "blood" should be retained.

At the Last Supper, when Jesus gives the bread and the cup to his disciples, he also reveals the symbolical meaning of the bread and the wine. The bread symbolizes his body, and the cup his blood (Mark 14:22-25; and parallels).

Leaven or yeast is mentioned several times in the NT as a symbol of evil. Jesus speaks of the leaven of the Pharisees, hypocrisy (Matt. 16:6). Paul exhorts the Corinthians to clean out the old leaven of evil (1 Cor.

5:6-8; cf. Exod. 12:15). On the other hand, Jesus can use leaven to symbolize the wonderful growth of the kingdom of heaven (Matt. 13:33).

In a similar fashion, the lion is a symbol of Christ, the "the Lion from the tribe of Judah" (Rev. 5:5), who then is seen as a slaughtered Lamb (5:6). On the other hand, Satan is said to go about like a roaring lion, seeking to devour God's people (1 Pet. 5:8).

The cloud is frequently used with a symbolical meaning. It can mean divine protection. The Israelites are under the cloud when they leave Egypt (1 Cor. 10:1). It is also a symbol of guidance (Exod. 13:21). When the Lord comes down at Sinai, he is in a thick cloud (Exod. 19:16). Daniel sees "one like a son of man" coming in the clouds of heaven (Dan. 7:13, RSV). The cloud, then, comes to symbolize God's hidden and majestic presence.

The final day of judgment is described as a day of clouds (Zeph. 1:15). Jesus will come with the clouds of heaven (Mark 14:62; Acts 1:9-11; Rev. 1:7). Clouds thus symbolize his majesty; they speak of both hiddenness and revelation.

There are many more material symbols that could be mentioned. We turn now to symbolical numbers.

Symbolical Numbers

Letters of the alphabet were used as numbers in Judaism. Important words, particularly names of people, were then sometimes given a numerical value. In Genesis 49:10 we have the promise of Shiloh. The numerical value of the consonants of *Shiloh* is 358. The word *Messiah* also has the same numerical value. So some rabbis concluded that *Shiloh* means *Messiah* (see the NRSV notes).

The numerical value of the word *Satan* is 364. Since

that is one day less than a full year, some interpreters suggested that on one day in each year, Satan could not do his evil work. Much of this is comical and meaningless. However, in a few biblical texts, the numerical value of a word may have some significance.

The consonants of the name *David* have a numerical value of 14 (D = 4, V = 6, D = 4). Scholars have often pointed out that in Matthew 1, where Christ is counted as the son of David (Matt. 1:1), the apostle gives the genealogy in three paragraphs of fourteen names each, perhaps to symbolize the name *David*.

When John wrote Revelation, it was probably too dangerous to mention by name the beast that persecuted the Christians. Hence, he uses the number 666 as a cover-up. He expects the readers to understand who is meant (Rev. 13:18), but outsiders may not (cf. 17:18, avoiding the name but meaning Rome).

No one knows for certain which evil personage John had in mind when he gave the beast this number, but Nero may be a good candidate. *Caesar Neron* yields 666 when the consonants are converted into numbers (if the spelling is *Nero*, the number is 616, as found in a variant manuscript reading).

We should not try to get 666 out of the name of every evil ruler that comes upon the scene. John was thinking of a Roman ruler who persecuted the believers. Evil rulers are found throughout human history and are forerunners and types of the one whom John in his epistles calls "antichrist" (1 John 2:18).

The church carries out its mission in the world between Christ's first coming and his coming at the end of the age. Thus, the church is symbolized by the two witnesses (Rev. 11). As a result of its mission efforts, the church often is persecuted. The length of this time of persecution is said to be three and a half years. *Three and a half years* becomes a symbolical number for the entire interim between Christ's first and second coming.

The concept goes back to Daniel 7:25; 12:7. In the second century B.C., the Syrian ruler Antiochus Epiphanes tried to stamp out Judaism. This led to terrible oppression for three and a half years (cf. the drought in Elijah's day, James 5:17). Three and a half years, then, becomes a symbolical number for the suffering of God's people, which God limits.

This number is also found in the form of forty-two months or 1,260 days (Rev. 11:2-3). Both the ministry of the two witnesses and the suffering of the church are said to last three and a half years, a symbolic number meaning from Pentecost to parousia.

In the OT the number *forty* is used so often that it becomes a symbolical number. The life of Moses is divided into three forties. Jews today still wish each other, "May you live to 120," meaning, "May you have a full life like Moses." It is remarkable how often the number 40 does occur.

At the time of the Flood, it rained for 40 days and nights. Israel was in the wilderness for 40 years. The spies were in the land of Canaan for 40 days. The judges in Israel were to give no more than 40 lashes. Moses was on the mountain for 40 days. Elijah was in the wilderness for 40 days. In 40 days Nineveh was to be destroyed.

The number 40 is used often for a time of distress and testing. That may play into the meaning of the temptation of Jesus in the wilderness for 40 days. But the symbolism of 40 days need not rule out the mathematical meaning.

Seven is given a specially sacred character among various peoples of the ancient Near East. This is likely related to the sun, moon, and five planets known to the ancients, and to the week of seven days, about a quarter of the lunar month.

Thus, in the Bible, the Sabbath is on the seventh day (Gen. 2:3; Exod. 20:10). God's people wait for the coming Sabbath rest (Heb. 4:9). After a series of sabbatical years, the Jubilee comes on the year after seven times seven years (Lev. 25). The spirit of the Lord is sevenfold, signifying completeness (Isa. 11:2-3, with the Septuagint adding "piety"; Rev. 1:4; 5:6). There are seven lamps on a holy lampstand (Exod. 25:31-40), and seven churches are addressed by the exalted Christ (Rev. 1–3).

Moses gathers *seventy* elders (Num. 11). Israel was in captivity seventy years (2 Chron. 36:31). Jesus sends out the seventy (Luke 10:1), thus symbolizing that the gospel is for all the nations of the world, then popularly counted as seventy. Jesus helps his disciples catch 153 fish (the sum of digits 1 to 17, one of several theories). This likely symbolizes the breadth and universality of the mission Jesus is assigning to his followers (John 21).

Twelve is a sign of the corporate people of God (Rev. 7:5-8). It fits the twelve patriarchs and tribes of Israel, and the twelve apostles (21:12-14). These are a few examples of numbers used in a symbolic fashion.

Symbolical Names

After Jacob has wrestled with a mysterious opponent at the Jabbok River, he receives a new name. He is to be called not Jacob, but Israel (Gen. 32:28), because he has striven with God and humans and has prevailed. Naomi asks to be called "Mara" because "the Almighty has dealt bitterly with me" (Ruth 1:20).

The wife of the prophet Isaiah bears a son, and she is to call him *Maher-shalal-hash-baz* (the spoil speeds, the prey hastes). Before the child will know how to call "My father" or "My mother," the wealth of Damascus and the spoil of Samaria will be carried away by the king of Assyria (Isa. 7–8).

The prophet Hosea is told to call his first son Jezreel. Though this is a place name, from the days of Jehu it has symbolized the shedding of blood. Hosea's son's name is to symbolize God's judgment on Jehu's successors, the kingship of the house of Israel.

Hosea's second child, a daughter, is to be called *Lo-Ruhamah* (no mercy), because God will no longer have mercy on Israel A second son is to be called *Lo-ammi* (no people), for apostate Israel is no longer God's people (Hos. 1:4-9).

The prophet is told, however, that a day will come when God will renew his covenant with his people. The apostle Peter sees the fulfillment of this promise in the new people of God: "Once you were not my people, but now you are God's people; once you had not received mercy, but now you have received mercy" (1 Pet. 2:10).

Jesus is given the symbolical name "Emmanuel" (Matt. 1:22-23; on this text, see chapter 12, below). This fulfills Isaiah's promise of a child's birth signifying that "God is with us" (Isa. 7:14).

In the book of Revelation, "Babylon" is the symbolical name for evil world powers standing in opposition to God and his people. Babylon is also a code term for Rome, for in John's day it had become an anti-Christian power. In 17:9 (cf. 17:18), the seven heads of the beast on which the Babylonian harlot sits are the "seven hills" of Rome (in Latin called *septicollis,* the seven-hilled city).

Godless Jerusalem is where our Lord was crucified and the witnesses of Jesus are persecuted and killed. It receives the symbolical names of "Sodom" and "Egypt," where God's people were mistreated and enslaved (Rev. 11:8).

God's armies and the forces of evil assemble for battle at "Harmagedon" (Rev. 16:16; KJV: Armageddon). Harmagedon cannot be found on any map; it is a symbolical name for the final showdown between God and his enemies. *Har* is the Hebrew word for mountain, and Megiddo is a valley where some of the many battles of Israel's history were fought. Megiddo then becomes a symbolic name for the last battle.

Why the word *mountain* is connected with it, is not quite clear. The valley of Megiddo does run into the Carmel range. The tell (mound of ruins) of Megiddo rises about seventy feet above the plain. Since Harmagedon is a symbolical name, we should not try to locate the last battle somewhere in modern Israel.

Symbolical Colors

In looking for the symbolism of colors, we must be cautious. We do not have to think of the blood of Christ every time the color *red* occurs. That holds true also for the red cord that Rahab hung over the wall in Jericho (Josh. 2:18), and in the case of the ashes of the red heifer (Num. 19:2).

The matter is quite different, however, when the four apocalyptic horses are given different colors that suggest their missions. The white horse stands for militarism, the red for bloodshed, the black for famine, and the pale-green for death. The interpretation of the colors is given to us by John, and so we know what they symbolize (Rev. 6:1-8).

The color *white* is frequently mentioned in the Bible. It speaks, for example, of purity (Isa. 1:18), but also of victory (Rev. 6:11; 7:9; 19:11-14). Generally speaking, white is the color of heaven (Rev. 3:4).

Purple is the color of royalty and high class (cf. Acts 16:14). When the soldiers mocked our Lord's kingship, they put a purple robe on him (Mark 15:17). The rich man in the parable clothed himself in purple and fine linen (Luke 16:19). The woman (Rome) on the beast was clothed in purple and scarlet (Rev. 17:4, 18).

Symbolism of Metals

Certain metals are mentioned repeatedly and acquire a symbolical meaning. Gold, of course, stands for what is most precious. Thus the street of the heavenly Jerusalem is to be of pure gold (Rev. 21:21), and so is the entire city (21:18). The same goes for the precious jewels (21:19-21).

Peter speaks of a tested faith as more precious than gold (1 Pet. 1:7). Silver and gold, however, cannot procure our redemption (1 Pet. 1:18-19). On the other hand, if the work we do on earth is to stand God's fiery test, we must build with gold, silver, and precious stones (1 Cor. 3:12-14). Wood, hay, and stubble represent what is combustible, ephemeral, and worthless.

Nebuchadnezzar has a dream in which he sees a statue with a golden head, breast and arms of silver, middle and thighs of bronze, legs of iron, and feet of iron and clay (Dan. 2:27-45). These metals represent the gradual deterioration of the kingdoms of this world, following Nebuchadnezzar's day. In the end, the stone that God cuts from the mountain strikes the feet, and the statue falls to the ground, as all earthly kingdoms eventually will. Only God's kingdom endures.

Because iron is a hard metal, it symbolizes strength and authority. There was a time when the Philistines harassed Israel by retaining a monopoly on making and sharpening iron tools (1 Sam. 13:19-22). According to Psalm 2:9, the Lord has appointed a king on Zion who is to judge the nations by breaking them to pieces with a rod of iron.

In the NT, the son born of the heavenly woman shall "shepherd all the nations with an iron rod" (Rev 12:5,

NRSV note). Out of the mouth of the heavenly ruler comes a sword (a word of judgment) with which he strikes down the nations, and he shepherds them with a rod of iron (19:15, NRSV note). The overcomers are granted a share of such authority (2:27; cf. 5:10; 22:5).

In all these references, the iron rod is a symbol of government or judgment. God is establishing his eternal kingdom on the ashes of the kingdoms of this world. The saints participate in this eternal reign of God.

The Bible uses many kinds of symbols and symbolism. Interpreters need to take these into account in a way that plays fair with the character of Scripture and the way the writers were thinking.

8

General Principles of Interpretation

From the long history of biblical studies and from their own experience, careful students of the Scriptures have discovered some general principles of interpretation. When Bible readers observe them, they avoid some serious misunderstandings of the text. These guidelines have become common knowledge in the Christian church. Bible students all over the world have found them to be useful.

As mentioned earlier, these hermeneutical guidelines have sometimes been compared to the rules of a game. A person might, for example, memorize the rules of tennis and yet not be able to play the game. Similarly, Bible readers might have a theoretical knowledge of the principles of interpretation, and yet not be adept at exegeting a biblical text. Students have to be constantly engaged in Bible study and have to play the game, if the rules of the game are to be meaningful. The following principles may help students of the Scriptures in understanding and applying the biblical message.

Interpret the Bible Literally
After all we have said about figurative language, this statement may come as a surprise and perhaps even

seem to be a contradiction. But we need to explain the meaning here of the word *literal*. We are talking about the *plain sense*, not about a wooden literalness. After all, Paul says that "the letter kills but the Spirit gives life" (2 Cor. 3:6).

An example of rigid literalism might be the prohibition against photography, based on the biblical injunction against making "any likeness of any thing . . . that is on the earth" (Exod. 20:4, KJV). Some might claim that Christians should not have household pets because Paul writes, "Beware of the dogs" (Phil. 3:2).

By literal interpretation, we mean that we must always seek to establish what the author of a biblical text wanted to say. We should look for the plain meaning and intent of the writer, who may be using a figure of speech or making a simple factual statement.

In every language, numerous words have generally accepted meanings. If that were not so, communication would be nearly impossible within any language group. We have names for objects (stick, foot, door), for activities (running, walking, eating), and for feelings (fear, hate, love). We have adverbs (quickly, slowly) and adjectives (beautiful, small, green), and we have abstract concepts (history, righteousness, power), and so forth.

However, in every language many familiar words have different meanings to match different contexts. When words occur in specific contexts in a given language, people usually know the meaning of these words or combination of words. This makes verbal communication possible.

So when we speak of literal interpretation, we mean that we understand the words of the text in a given context in their ordinary everyday sense. Figures of speech must also be interpreted literally. When a writer uses picture language, we ask, What did he want to say with that figure of speech?

When the lion is used to represent the devil, we can't understand that figure of speech unless we know literally that a lion is a dangerous and powerful beast. The symbolical meaning of Sarah and Hagar (Gal. 4:21-31) can be understood only if we know the story of these two women in a straightforward way.

In the early centuries of Christianity, we know of two chief schools of interpretation. The Alexandrian school tended toward allegorical exegesis; the Antiochian emphasized the literal interpretation of the Scriptures.

In the allegorical method, we do not ask what the biblical writer wanted to say. We simply take biblical truths from anywhere in Scripture and read them into a given text, hanging specific meanings onto minor details.

An example is how Augustine treated the good Samaritan parable (Luke 10:30-37). He said the traveler was Adam, expelled from the heavenly city of peace (Jerusalem) and heading for the moon (Jericho), the symbol of mortality. Others may admire the ingenuity of such an interpreter. Nevertheless, the allegorical method does not help us catch the literal meaning of what the biblical writer wanted to say.

Literal interpretation should also not be seen as a superficial reading of the Bible. Sometimes what passes for knowledge of the Scriptures is statistical knowledge. Some may know how many chapters are in each book of the Bible or which is the longest or the shortest chapter. They may have memorized long portions of Scripture and quote verses from OT and NT with ease. Yet it doesn't mean that such people have an understanding of the Bible's message.

Such an outward knowledge of the Bible is not

entirely useless, but it does not lead us into the meaning of the sacred writings. Literal interpretation means that we seek to grasp what the biblical writer wanted to convey in his day to his audience. After we do that, we must ask, How does this ancient message apply to our own lives today? That leads us to another general principle of hermeneutics.

Distinguish Interpretation and Application

The meanings of the words and sentences of the original writers of Holy Scripture never change; they are locked in history. Our first task as interpreters always is to establish the original meaning of a given text. After we have wrestled with what the prophet or apostle, guided by the Holy Spirit, wanted to communicate to his generation, we ask, What is God saying to us, to me, through this word of Scripture?

If we do not apply the Scriptures to our lives today, Bible study can become an academic exercise. As Paul puts it in Romans 15:4, "Whatever was written in former days was written for our instruction, so that by steadfastness and by the encouragement of the scriptures we might have hope."

In similar fashion, Paul writes to Timothy, "All scripture is inspired by God and is useful for teaching, for reproof, for correction, and for training in righteousness" (2 Tim. 3:16). Clearly the goal of all Bible studies is the edification of the reader. We are concerned, not only with the discovery of the literal meaning of a text, but also with its application to our lives.

A biblical text has basically only one meaning. Yet the application of it may vary, depending on the readers and their life situation. Isaiah stood in the temple and heard the Lord ask, "Whom shall I send, and who will go for us?" (6:8). That question had a specific meaning for the prophet. But when we read that same question today, it may be God asking us to go into the mission field or to devote our lives to helping the needy.

John the Baptist explained to his followers that he had to decrease, while Jesus had to increase (John 3:30). That explanation had a specific meaning at a given time in salvation history. John's disciples needed to know why people were leaving the Baptist and following Jesus. But what does it mean for us, when we read that statement today? James Stewart of Scotland once preached a powerful sermon on this text: "The Heroism of Self-Effacement" (74ff.).

Paul clearly warns his Ephesian readers not to be drunk with wine (Eph. 5:18). No great hermeneutical dexterity is required to understand that he is condemning intoxication (whether from wine, beer, vodka, or even drugs). But if that's not our problem, does the warning say nothing to us? It is legitimate to apply this prohibition to other areas of life: we may be caught up in ideas or practices that enslave us.

Paul tells the Galatian readers, who were putting stock in circumcision (Gal. 5:2), that circumcision did not contribute to their salvation. Salvation is by faith in the finished work of Christ alone. But that is likely not our problem. However, the text still applies to our situation when we discover that we are basing the assurance of our salvation on something we have done rather than on the grace of Christ alone.

How do we apply the command of Jesus to go into "all nations" and preach the gospel (Matt. 28:19-20)? The apostles understood this mandate literally and carried it out in their lifetime. In their day, "all nations" meant the Roman empire. How do *we* obey this command?

One person becomes a pastor, another a Christian

teacher, and another contributes generously to the work of God's kingdom. Still another is constantly in prayer for God's faithful witnesses. Others share their faith at their places of work or invest their lives in bringing relief to the hungry and oppressed. The application of Jesus' missionary mandate will vary from person to person.

Biblical narratives are probably easier to understand, but often more difficult to apply. How, for example, shall we apply the Joseph stories (Gen. 37ff.) to our lives today?

Some have interpreted them allegorically: We can see parallels between Joseph and Christ: Joseph was a shepherd, and so was Jesus. Joseph was loved by his father; so was Jesus. Joseph was hated by his brothers, and Jesus' brothers did not believe in him. Joseph got a bride from the Gentiles; so does Jesus (church as bride of Christ). Joseph triumphed over temptation; so did Jesus.

Such comparisons, however, add little to our understanding of the Joseph stories. They leave us cold, as far as application to our own lives is concerned. Yet we may ask, Why were Joseph's brothers angry with him? Probing into those family relations can help us learn something for our own lives. Joseph comes across as arrogant when he tells his brothers his dreams. That's a warning to us.

Parents might learn from the Joseph story not to give one child preferential treatment, as did Joseph's father. The story of Joseph's triumph over temptation is, of course, easily transferred. We can also learn from Joseph to be faithful wherever we are. Then there is his trust in God and his loyalty to his family. He forgave those who had so shamefully wronged him, demonstrating genuine godliness. No one reading that story can fail to see applications to our own lives.

Some years ago I heard Murdo Macdonald of Scotland preach a sermon on Job 41:1 (GNB), "Can you catch Leviathan with a fishhook?" In his introduction, Macdonald explained the meaning of that question in the context of the book of Job. He established that Leviathan here represents an evil power, too great for a human being to catch or tame. He began to apply this question to society today.

Macdonald mentioned a number of "hooks" (ways) through which people today try to overcome evils in our society, but with little success. In the end he proclaimed that God's grace is sufficient to tame the Leviathans in our own lives and in our society. Perhaps this was almost too ingenious!

Let us take the Advent text, "The virgin shall conceive and bear a son, and they shall name him Emmanuel" (Matt. 1:23). This is a quotation from Isaiah 7:14 (on these texts, see chap. 12, below). Hence, we have to establish, first, what it meant for the days of king Ahaz, in the eighth century B.C. Next, we must inquire what this angelic word meant in the case of Joseph, when he discovered that Mary was pregnant.

Finally we have to ask, What does this promise of "Emmanuel," that "God is with us," mean for us today in our circumstances? In the latter case, we are no longer dealing so much with interpretation as with application.

We should guard against making forced or bizarre applications of biblical passages. The apostle John sees a star fall from heaven, turning a third of the waters into wormwood (Rev. 8:10-11). He is not speaking of the pollution of our lakes and rivers in our day. The demonic locusts emerging from the abyss certainly do not refer to the French Revolution (Rev. 9:2-12). Likewise, the book John is asked to swallow is not a reference to the Protestant Reformation (Rev. 10:9-10, KJV).

The two witnesses can hardly be identified with Luther and Melanchthon (Rev. 11). Such applications are fanciful, do violence to the message of the apostle, and contribute nothing to believers' lives. On the other hand, these two witnesses may be seen as representatives of the church's witness. That witness leads to persecution and sometimes death, but ultimately to triumph in the heavenly kingdom. Then Christian readers in similar circumstances will be greatly encouraged.

It is fanciful to identify the three foul spirits coming out of the mouth of the dragon (Rev. 16:13) as Luther's opponents (Faber, Emser, and Eck) or as representing modern loudspeakers. But if they are understood as demonic spirits (as 16:14 explains), sent by Satan to deceive and harm humankind, we can apply this verse to our own situations. We can remind ourselves that we must put on the whole armor of God to stand against the wiles of the devil (Eph. 6:11).

We must, therefore, distinguish between interpretation and application. If we choose a wrong meaning for the text, we are bound to make a faulty application as well. However, we may understand the text correctly and still make an unwarranted application. Constant study of the Scriptures will give us a feel for interpretation *and* application.

Seek the More Natural Interpretation

We have just seen how meaningless the interpretation of a text can be when it is arbitrary and fanciful. If an interpretation is so complicated that it baffles all but a handful of experts, it probably is wrong. The Bible is not intended to be a book of puzzles, though it does have some passages difficult to understand.

We need to seek an interpretation that seems to flow more naturally out of the biblical passage and appears to be reasonable to readers or hearers. That is more likely to be correct or lead us in the right direction. Of course, what seems so natural and reasonable to one person may appear to be wrong to another. For example, some students of the Scriptures may know the original languages and be conversant with the history and cultures of the ancient world. What seems obvious to them may not be so obvious to students who do not have that kind of exegetical preparation.

Yet we must never forget that the books of the Bible were written for ordinary people, not for experts. Unsophisticated Bible readers have at times remarked that they find the Bible easier to understand than the commentaries designed to explain it.

Let us look at a few texts to illustrate what we mean by the more natural meaning of a passage! Take the petition in the Lord's Prayer, "Give us this day our daily bread" (Matt. 6:11), or "our bread for tomorrow" (NRSV note). We would think all readers could understand that petition. Even in countries where the staple diet is something other than bread made of flour, people know what it means to ask God for daily sustenance. Then they can sleep, assured of food for the coming day.

When we look at the history of the interpretation of the Lord's Prayer, however, we discover that this petition has not always been understood in its natural sense. Because the other petitions in the prayer express spiritual concerns, some interpreters felt that the prayer for daily bread had to be understood spiritually as well.

Augustine suggested that it referred to the bread of the Eucharist, "supersubstantial bread." Still others thought the petition expressed the longing of believers to have a share of the heavenly banquet in the eternal kingdom, and so forth. But surely the more natural interpretation is the correct one.

Jesus tells Simon Peter, in response to his confession, "You are Peter, and on this rock I will build my church" (Matt. 16:18). He is using metaphorical language, but the figure of speech (the church built on a firm foundation) is easy to understand. Yet some interpreters have constantly tried to avoid the natural meaning of the text because they do not want Jesus saying that Peter is the rock on which the church is built.

Peter, however, is the leader of the apostles, and he is only the representative of the Twelve. Paul also teaches that the church is built on the foundation of the apostles and prophets (Eph. 2:20). Since Protestant commentators want to set themselves off from Roman Catholic interpretations, they seem to be unable to let the text speak for itself. The passage, of course, has nothing to do with the Roman papacy.

Some Bible readers are firm believers in the eternal security of the saints. They have difficulty reading John 15:2, where Jesus speaks of branches on the vine that do not bear fruit: "He removes every branch in me that bears no fruit. Every branch that bears fruit, he prunes to make it bear more fruit." Jesus continues: "Whoever does not abide in me is thrown away like a branch and withers; such branches are gathered, thrown into the fire, and burned" (15:6).

Since these sayings of Jesus are hard to harmonize with the doctrine of eternal security, these passages have at times been given rather unnatural meanings. For example, some say that Christ removes the unfruitful branches from this earth and takes them into heaven. But the text says nothing of the sort. The cutoff branches are gathered and burned.

This text is a warning to believers. That doesn't mean that Christians live in constant fear that they may be lost. There are plenty of passages offering assurances of salvation for those who stay loyal to Jesus. But we should not force the verses just mentioned to say something they do not say.

Peter says that Christ bore our sins in his body to the cross, and "by his wounds you have been healed" (1 Pet. 2:24). He means that our sins are now forgiven and we have been restored to wholeness. Since sin is sometimes spoken of as a sickness, forgiveness of sins is called healing, as in Psalm 103:1-3: "Bless the Lord, . . . who forgives all your iniquity, who heals all your diseases." That is the natural meaning of this wonderful word of assurance.

Nevertheless, some interpret this text to mean that believers, who have experienced the benefits of Christ's work on the cross, can claim healing now from any physical disease or sickness.

We reply: Sickness does not need to be atoned for; it needs to be removed. Because of Christ's work on the cross, it will be removed someday. When believers experience physical healing now, they have a foretaste of freedom from sickness. However, we have not yet entered the eternal kingdom, where sickness and death are not known (Rev. 21:4).

Interpret Difficult Texts in Light of the Scriptures as a Whole

At the time of the Protestant Reformation, it was often said that the Scriptures interpret themselves (*scriptura sacra sui ipsius interpres*). The Reformers wanted to underscore the clarity of the Bible's message. The medieval church hierarchy claimed that it alone had the right to give the proper interpretation of the Bible's teachings. On the other hand, the Reformers insisted that believers could go directly to the Word of God. They didn't need to filter the message of the Bible through the doctrinal grid of the Roman Catholic Church.

That conviction moved Martin Luther to give the German-speaking people the Bible in their mother tongue. Of course, not everything in the Scriptures is completely plain. Everyone who reads the Bible knows that it contains some difficult parts. Yet such passages should not be used to formulate teachings that run counter to the message of the Bible as a whole. Instead, they should be understood in the light of the entire Bible.

To understand the Bible as a whole, we do have to study its parts. This is sometimes called the "hermeneutical circle"—the whole is understood in terms of its parts, and the parts must be understood in light of the whole. Hence, there will be some back-and-forth movement when we grapple with texts that do not immediately yield a satisfactory meaning.

Let us take another illustration from the Lord's Prayer. Jesus teaches his disciples to pray, "Lead us not into temptation" (Matt. 6:13, KJV). But why such a petition? Would God ever lead his children into temptation? To answer such questions, we need to look at other parts of the Bible.

The apostle James assures us (1:13) that God never tempts anyone to do evil. This clear statement suggests, then, that the prayer "Lead us not into temptation" does not mean that God *tempts* his children to do evil.

We gain another perspective in the first book of the Bible. Genesis reports that God "did tempt" Abraham (22:1, KJV) by commanding him to sacrifice his son, Isaac. In light of the outcome of the story, we understand, that "did tempt" meant "tested" (as in NRSV). God wanted to see whether Abraham would obey him.

With these two perspectives, we can now more easily understand the petition, "Lead us not into temptation." It is a confession of our own weakness. We cry out for God's help; we don't have the strength in ourselves to stand firm in the testing and trials of life that God in his providence allows to come our way. When testing comes, we claim the promise that God will faithfully "provide the way out" (1 Cor. 10:13).

It is not easy for believers to systematize passages of the NT that seem to speak of the end times. However, there is an overarching unity in the eschatology of the apostolic writers. If, then, one passage describes the coming of our Lord at the end of this age in somewhat different language than does another, we should not immediately jump to the conclusion that there must be more than one coming of Jesus.

According to 1 Thessalonians 4:13-18, Christ will come from heaven to receive his church. This coming is sometimes called "the rapture," because of the verb "caught up" (4:17), translated by the Latin Vulgate as *rapere* (to seize, snatch). When we come to 2 Thessalonians 1:7-10, where the coming of the Lord is also described, we are given a somewhat different picture of his return at the end of the age.

In Revelation 7 and 14, the saints are described as coming home to the heavenly Mount Zion. The Lord does not come to get them and bring them home to glory. In chapter 19, Christ does come with great power and majesty, but he comes to put down all evil powers in rebellion against God.

On one hand, the day of the Lord is a glorious day; on the other, it is a day of judgment (Amos 5:20). The different portrayals of Christ's coming at the end of the age all refer to the same event. So when some claim that Christ comes first "for" the saints and then again "with" the saints, we are going beyond the bounds of Scripture.

Sometimes people ask, What will heaven be like?

The NT also gives us various answers on this, and we should not pit one against the other. Instead, we may think of them as different ways of speaking of the same glorious place to which all believers hope to go. Jesus spoke of heaven as his Father's house, with many rooms (John 14:2). In the parable of the rich man and Lazarus, Lazarus is carried by the angels into "Abraham's bosom." This is a Semitic description of heavenly bliss.

Jesus also spoke of believers being received into "the eternal tents" (Luke 16:9). In a few passages, heaven is called "paradise" (as in Luke 23:43; Rev. 2:7). In Revelation 21:18, the eternal home of Christ's followers is described as a city of gold. In Revelation 22:1-4, it is portrayed as a restored paradise.

These are all figures of speech. Such superterrestrial realities can be understood by human beings, with their limited horizons, only by analogies taken from this life. What is important is that we take all of these images into account and not draw a picture of heaven on the basis of one passage alone.

To catch a fuller view of a biblical doctrine, it is often helpful to study parallel passages, as we have just done. If, for example, we want to understand the doctrine of justification by faith, we should begin with Genesis 15 and 17. We see that Abraham was justified by faith. From there, we may go to Habakkuk 2:3-4, where the prophet speaks in similar categories.

In the NT, we will want to pursue this doctrine particularly in Paul's letters to the Galatians (3:11) and to the Romans (1:17). However, to get a more comprehensive understanding of this teaching, we have to take into account Hebrews 10:38. How do these writers use Habakkuk 2:3-4? We must particularly take note of what James has to say about justification by faith or by works (2:14-26).

Difficult passages must be seen in the light of the teachings of the Bible as a whole. They may not always be explained by parallel passages. But parallel passages will at least give us perspectives that keep us from deriving false doctrines from these difficult texts.

How, for example, are we to understand the notoriously difficult passage in Genesis 6? The sons of God saw that the daughters of men were fair, and they took wives for themselves of all that they chose (6:1-2). Recently when a man asked me what I thought the passage meant, I gave him several possible meanings:

• The sons of God may be descendants of Seth, and the daughters descendants of the ungodly line of Cain. What we have, then, is the intermarriage of the godly and the ungodly.

• Sons of God may be a reference to princes and kings building up their harems, in typical oriental fashion. They take one pretty woman after another for themselves.

• Sons of God and daughters of men may be two ways of speaking about people made in the image of God (sons of God; cf. Gen. 1:26; Luke 3:38), but who are human (daughters of men), not divine. The evil was that the men were carried away by lust and practiced polygamy—a violation of the creation order (Gen. 2:24).

• Sons of God here may be angelic or divine beings (Job 1:6, KJV; Ps. 82; the audience of Gen. 1:26; 3:22; 11:7). They come to earth and marry fair maidens, threatening to mix the divine and the human. Yet human beings remain mortal (6:3; some later, noncanonical Jewish writings traced the origin of evil and of fallen divine beings to Gen. 6:1-4; see Roop).

I did not commend this last interpretation to my questioner because it seemed like typical pagan mythology of gods cohabiting with humans. But that was precisely the interpretation preferred by my questioner, who ended the conversation. The various interpretations I suggested made no sense to him. Perhaps I should have reminded him of what Jesus said about angels, in answering the Sadducees (Mark 12:25). When people get to heaven, he said, they are like angels and do not marry.

Some Bible readers find it puzzling to hear what Jesus says to his disciples, in the face of his imminent arrest: "The one who has no sword must sell his cloak and buy one" (Luke 22:36). That exhortation must be seen in the light of Jesus' teaching of nonviolence as found, for example, in the Sermon on the Mount (Matt. 5:38-48).

Jesus' actions point in the same direction. He lets himself be arrested, and he heals the ear that Peter cut off while defending Jesus with the sword. Jesus speaks his disapproval of Peter's use of the sword (Matt. 26:51-54; Luke 22:47-51).

When the disciples assure Jesus that they have two swords, Jesus responds, "Enough of that" discussion (Luke 22:38, author's trans.) They have misunderstood his metaphorical use of the word "sword" and think the kingdom of God can be advanced with physical weapons. Jesus is not encouraging armed conflict; he is urging them to be mentally and spiritually ready to face hostility. Later Jesus tells Pilate that if his "kingdom were from this world," his followers would fight (John 18:36).

One of the difficult passages in the NT is 1 Peter 3:18-20. The text says that Christ "was put to death in the flesh, but made alive in the spirit, in which also he went and made a proclamation to the spirits in prison, who in former times did not obey, when God waited patiently in the days of Noah." Several questions arise:
  • Who were the spirits in prison? Were they fallen

angels? Were they OT saints?
- What did Christ proclaim? Was he offering them a second chance to repent? Was he proclaiming his completed work of salvation? Was he announcing their judgment?
- When did Christ make this proclamation? In the days of Noah? Between his death and his resurrection? After his resurrection?

We see, then, that this passage bristles with an array of hermeneutical pitfalls. Equally qualified exegetes have not agreed on the meaning of this passage, at least not on the details. Sometimes we can only give possible interpretations and let it go at that. Erland Waltner opts for this being Christ's proclamation of victory over the spirit world.

In the light of what the Bible as a whole teaches on life beyond death, we should not infer from this passage that God gives people who reject him here in life another chance after death. Blaise Pascal observed that the Bible has enough light to enlighten the elect, but also enough mystery to keep them humble. That would certainly apply to this Petrine passage.

These discussions illustrate the importance of interpreting individual passages of Scripture in the light of the whole. In conclusion, we add the following:
- The main doctrines of the Bible should be based on texts that are clear.
- Exegesis comes before doctrine. In other words, exegesis must not be determined by doctrine.
- Doctrinal formulations should not go beyond what the biblical text allows.
- No fundamental doctrine should be built on a single passage of the Bible.

Interpret in Community with Others, Testing the Result by Life's Experiences

This is not a criticism of private Bible study, which we greatly encourage. Nevertheless, our understanding of the Scriptures needs to be tested in dialogue with other Bible readers. It is therefore quite helpful if one can be a part of a Bible study fellowship.

Bible readers normally also attend the worship services of some church and will receive instruction from the Word of God in that setting. In most churches, the Scriptures are studied also in the Christian education department of the church. In all these settings, we can gain perspectives on how to interpret the Bible.

Even if you cannot be part of a Bible study group or a Bible class, there is a way of comprehending the Scriptures "together with all God's people" (Eph. 3:18, GNB). We can use helpful tools in the private study of the Bible. You might have a good Bible dictionary at hand, a concordance, a few translations of the Bible, and above all, a few good commentaries. The commentaries will not always agree with each other, but they will keep us from making serious blunders in understanding the text.

A few books on the customs of people in Bible times would also help us grasp the message of the Scriptures more easily. Some knowledge of church history, particularly the history of Christian thought, helps to give us perspectives in our reading of the Bible.

Biblical teachings need to be tested in everyday life. For example, we might come to the conclusion that as believers we no longer sin (and we can find passages that speak of Christian perfection). If we do so, we have not read the Bible correctly.

First of all, we are explicitly told that if we make such a claim, we deceive ourselves (1 John 1:8). But Christian experience also denies perfectionism. We rejoice in the forgiveness of our sins. We also experience victory over evil tendencies in our lives by the help of the Spirit of God. But we all know that we are still prone to sin.

The history of the church provides many examples of people who made bold claims of having attained Christian perfection, but who gave little evidence of this in everyday life. Perfectionism is simply not true to Christian experience. (Of course, satisfaction with imperfection is also perverse.)

In some Christian circles, the Bible has been interpreted to teach that Christians should not and need not be poor. This is sometimes called the "health and wealth doctrine." Such a teaching may not be a problem in some rich communities of North America, but it is quite problematic in Calcutta. All over the world, believers are suffering because they lack necessities of daily life. That is due, not to their lack of spirituality, but to the bad social and economic systems with which they have to contend.

This teaching, that God's children need not be poor, is often based on the OT law of retribution. God promised the Israelites that if they would remain true to the covenant, he would bless them materially (and vice versa, as in Deut. 28). This promise created great problems for OT saints when fair retribution did not seem to function in an individual's life and the righteous suffered (like Job).

NT believers may try to claim that since they are children of Abraham, they, like Abraham, should also be blessed with material goods. But that is a misunderstanding of what the apostles mean when they call believers "children of Abraham." There is not a single passage in the NT that guarantees the followers of Jesus material prosperity. This teaching must, then, be rejected, because it is not borne out by the everyday experiences of believers.

The same must be said of the teaching that believers should not have to suffer physical ailments if they claim Christ's healing power. We agree that God does heal his children from time to time in extraordinary ways. But there is nothing in Scripture that guarantees health now to the followers of Jesus.

Moreover, everyday life does not bear out this teaching that believers need not suffer. Believers all over the world get sick and die, without experiencing miraculous healing. The apostle John wishes that his friend Gaius might experience physical well-being, "just as it is well with your soul" (3 John 2; cf. 2 Cor. 12:7). This certainly is no guarantee that either he or anyone else will always be physically well.

In eschatology, another area of biblical teaching, experience has repeatedly proved that the Scriptures have been misinterpreted. Throughout the history of the Christian church, preachers and Bible teachers have set dates for the second coming of Christ. Thus far, such dates have all proved to be wrong. Yet people continue to set dates for the end of the age.

Usually they set those dates on the basis of political, social, or economic developments, with Bible verses thrown in to make the prognostications more believable. But Jesus said that no one knows the day or the hour when Christ will return (Mark 13:32). After so many unfulfilled predictions, people could learn not to project time lines for the end of this age. Experience teaches us not to indulge in such speculations.

Taking Texts Seriously on Both Sides

Let us check article 20 of the Thirty-Nine Articles, the sixteenth-century historical doctrinal standard of the

Church of England: "It is not lawful for the Church to ordain anything that is contrary to God's Word written, neither may it expound one place of Scripture, that may be repugnant to another."

There are biblical texts that seem to move in opposite directions. In such cases, we should not conclude that we have to contend with contradictions. Different biblical writers (or even a single writer) may simply be stressing different aspects of the believers' lives or, perhaps, addressing people in different life situations.

For example, the Scriptures assure us that God will keep us safely in his hands until we enter the gates of glory (as in 1 Pet. 1:5). On the other hand, the apostles repeatedly warn Christians against sin and apostasy.

In his letter to the Philippians, Paul assures his readers that the One who began the good work in them will also complete it on the day of Jesus Christ (1:6). But in the next chapter, he exhorts them to work out their salvation with fear and trembling (2:12-13). It is not easy to put these two emphases on a common denominator, and the controversies over the teaching of the preservation of the believer bear this out.

Leaning heavily on Augustine stressing the sovereignty of God, John Calvin taught that the elect (chosen by God) were eternally secure. Jacob Arminius, however, had serious questions about this one-sided emphasis and taught that believers could in fact apostatize and no longer be believers. From the sixteenth century to the present, entire denominations have identified with either of these two positions.

John Wesley and George Whitefield both played an important role in the revivals of the eighteenth century in the English-speaking world. Yet they were at odds over this question. Wesley tended toward Arminianism, and Whitefield toward Calvinism.

How then should we handle such apparently contradictory emphases in the Scriptures? We should take
both emphases seriously, without trying to force them
logically into an artificial harmony. For example, we
take seriously all the passages that assure us of God's
keeping power. But we also take seriously the warnings
of Scripture against a life of sin, rebellion against God,
and apostasy. We need both of these emphases.

When we feel our sinfulness and our moral weakness so keenly, we need to hear the words of Jesus that
no one will snatch us out of his hands (John 10:28-29).
When we become careless and indifferent, we had better listen also to the warnings of the Bible.

Perhaps a figure of speech can help us see this. God
does not build walls around us to keep us from tum-
bling down the cliff. He builds wills within us, so that
we won't go too close to the edge. The Scriptures assure
us of our perseverance and warn us against the power
of evil. When we take both of these emphases seriously,
God keeps us safe and helps us enter the heavenly kingdom.

Martin Luther found a serious contradiction between
Paul and James. Paul stresses justification by faith;
James speaks of justification by works with faith (James
2:24). Luther's favorite epistles were Romans and
Galatians, where justification by faith is so clearly
taught. He disliked the epistle of James and called it "a
right strawy epistle." Luther confessed that he was
tempted to throw James into the Elbe River. He even
offered his doctor's beret to anyone who would harmonize Paul and James.

Here again, the contradiction between these two
epistles is only apparent; it is not real. Paul also puts
great emphasis on good works—not as grounds for salvation, for that is a gift of God's grace, but as evidence

of a genuine faith (Eph. 2:8-10). That is precisely what James is trying to underscore. We are not true to Scripture when we pit faith against works; we must take both seriously.

Another example of an apparently contradictory emphasis is Paul's teaching on the ministry of Christian women. From 1 Corinthians 11, we would have to conclude that the woman had the same freedom to pray and prophesy in the public worship services of the early church as did the man (assuming that she observed the laws of propriety in dress).

When we come to 1 Corinthians 14, however, it seems as if Paul takes away some of this freedom from the woman: "As in all the churches of the saints, women should be silent in the churches. For they are not permitted to speak, but should be subordinate, as the law also says" (14:33-34).

How shall these two emphases be reconciled? We can't simply accept chapter 11 and reject chapter 14, or the other way round. Let me illustrate ways in which interpreters have wrestled with this dual emphasis:

• In chapter 11, Paul has the informal meetings of the church in mind; in chapter 14 the regular worship service. The woman has the freedom to speak at the former, but not at the latter. Reply: This interpretation fails because we know nothing of such differences in the meetings of the early church.

• Praying and prophesying are simply idiomatic for full participation in the worship of the church. This is in contrast to the Jewish synagogue, where women were not full participants. It doesn't mean that women actually prayed or prophesied (chap. 11). Reply: It appears from the NT that they did. We think, for example, of the daughters of Philip (Acts 21:8-9).

• Women had the freedom to pray and prophesy like

men, but they were not to speak in tongues, lest they add to the confusion in worship. Reply: While it is true that chapter 14 deals with speaking in tongues versus prophesying, the command to keep silent does not seem to be limited to speaking in tongues. Paul also says, "Do not forbid speaking in tongues" (14:39).

• In chapter 11 Paul had single women in mind, whereas in chapter 14 he addresses married women. Married women were to demonstrate their submission to their husbands by not speaking in public. Reply: There is no indication in chapter 11 that Paul is restricting his instructions to single women. In fact, quite the opposite seems to be the case: "the husband is the head of his wife" (11:3).

• The prohibition against speaking in public has nothing to do with praying and prophesying. Instead, since men and women (with small children) sat separately, women tended to chat among themselves and disturb the worship service. In other words, Paul's prohibition against women speaking may mean that they were not to carry on casual conversations when the church gathered in some home for worship. Reply: Plausible.

• The exhortation to keep silent has to do with testing what the prophets say (14:29). By giving her opinion on what was said, she might not be subordinate to her husband. Reply: There is no indication in the text (14:34) that the speaking Paul forbids means testing what the prophets say. The questions might have been for simple clarification.

• Several evangelical scholars, including Gordon Fee (699-708), hold that 14:34-35 is a marginal gloss (addition) inserted by a Judaizer, perhaps as early as the late first century. If so, it is an attempt to keep women from exercising their newfound freedom in Christ. The

Western family of manuscripts has this restrictive passage after 14:40, because verses 34-35 seem to disrupt the argument of the entire chapter. These scholars claim that internal and external evidence mark this as a non-Pauline passage; they feel no need to try to establish a harmony between chapters 11 and 14. Reply: Yet 14:34-35 is still in our Bible for us to interpret.

• Still another approach suggests that 14:34-35 presents a quotation from the letter the Corinthians have sent Paul (as in 7:1; 8:1). It might restate the view of some Corinthians, such as the Cephas party, who wanted to impose certain restrictions on Christian women. Then 14:36-38 is seen as Paul's response to this kind of imposition of "the Law" on the church. Reply: Though Paul does respond here and there to what (some of) the Corinthians were saying, there is no precedent for such a long quotation (14:34-35), to which the apostle responds.

• Paul forbids women to ask questions during the service. He does not forbid them to pray or to prophesy. Such an interpretation could be gleaned from the comment that, if they have questions, they are to ask their husbands when they get home (on differing educational levels, see below). Reply: Plausible.

• The command to keep silent in the church is culture bound. In that early period of the Christian church, it would not have been acceptable for women to have the same freedom to speak in public that men had. Moreover, girls did not normally attend school, as did boys. Paul wants Christian women to be informed (they are to "learn," 14:35). Once they have made progress in that area, they will have greater freedom to speak (11:5). Reply: Plausible.

In my opinion, Paul did not want the church to come into disrepute by allowing women to exercise a freedom they did not normally exercise in the society of that day. Thus it follows that in a culture where it is perfectly acceptable for women to speak in public, Christian women may also pray and prophesy like men.

The above is a lengthy discussion of ways in which the apparent discrepancy between 1 Corinthians 11 and 14 has been handled. It is not designed to settle the question of how much freedom the Christian woman has in the exercise of her gifts. I simply wanted to illustrate how Bible scholars have to wrestle with texts when they seem to be going in opposite directions.

Martin Luther apparently was untroubled by such so-called irreconcilable discrepancies in the Bible. He suggested, "Let it pass; it does not endanger the articles of the Christian faith" (via Goldingay, 1995:263). Such an attitude should, however, not be understood as an excuse for failure to wrestle seriously with such apparent discrepancies. As we have just mentioned, Luther felt quite differently about what appeared in his eyes to be a contradiction between Paul and James.

These general principles of biblical interpretation may help all students of the Scriptures to understand and apply the biblical message in the community of faith, when gathered and when scattered.

9

Cultural Settings of the Bible

The world of the Bible is not our world, and the world of the Bible is not uniform. After all, the books of the Bible were written over a long period of time. The world changed a lot between Moses and the apostle John.

Our world is also not uniform. Africa is not North America; Europe is not Asia. Even within Europe, there is great cultural diversity. But what do we mean when we speak of culture? Sometimes we use the word *culture* for the finer or more sophisticated aspects of people's lives, such as poetry, music, drama, art, and the like. However, the word *culture* is also used in the anthropological sense, particularly in the language of missiology, to designate the customs and practices of different people groups.

This chapter uses *culture* in the broader anthropological sense: it embraces people's treatment of the environment (agriculture, technology, etc.); how human beings order their social and physical relationships in a given society (law, marriage, etc.); and how humans in a given people group relate to one another intellectually and spiritually (language, knowledge, religion, ideology, etc.).

In the past, some serious errors have been made in

translating and interpreting the Scriptures. Many mistakes happened because students did not take into account the deep gap between the cultures of the Bible and the cultures of later Bible readers. The Scriptures must be interpreted culturally. That unsettles some Bible students who think that if we adapt the message of the Bible to our culture, we can make it say what we wish. That is not the case.

The message of the Bible is for all times, but it has come to us in ancient clothing. We want to retain the living Word of God. To do so, we must take careful account of the Bible's ancient dress. Then we can faithfully reclothe the biblical message, putting it into forms with which we are familiar.

Our task would be much simpler if all the books of the Bible reflected the same cultural dress, but that is not the case. We must reckon with the culture of Canaan at the time of the Patriarchs. Then there is the Egyptian culture, since Israel lived in Egypt for 430 years. Moreover, Israel also had to deal with smaller and greater powers—Syria, Assyria, Babylonia, and Persia.

Then the community of the Jews who returned from the exile had to face the Hellenistic rulers of Syria to the north and Egypt to the south. Finally, by the time the books of the NT came to be written, Rome ruled the known world. We cannot describe in detail the customs and practices of these different cultures. But let us look at a few aspects of the cultural dimensions that are reflected in the books of the NT (perhaps with a few pointers to the OT).

Material Culture

The houses in Jesus' day reflect the material culture of his times. Most of them had but one room, illuminated by an oil lamp. The door opened directly onto the street.

At night, the sleeping mats were spread out on the floor. Thus in the parable of the friend at midnight, the householder responded, "The door has already been locked, and my children are with me in bed; I cannot get up and give you anything" (Luke 11:7).

Houses were often built without foundations. That made it possible for thieves to dig through (Matt. 6:20). Jesus compared the house built on the rock with one built on sand (Matt. 7:24-27).

Because the houses had flat roofs, each had an outside ladder that led to the roof. That explains why the four friends who brought the paralyzed man to Jesus went onto the roof, dug it open, and lowered the man into the presence of Jesus (Mark 2:1-12).

Larger houses often had an extra boxlike second story, called "the upper room" (Luke 22:12). Jesus ate the Last Supper with his disciples in such an upper room. The 120 gathered in an upper story before Pentecost (Acts 1:13-15). The upper room was sometimes used as a guesthouse. In Acts 10:5-6, Peter stayed in the upper room of Simon the Tanner. Some knowledge of houses in Jesus' day helps us understand certain biblical passages.

The same can be said about daily labor. Working with the hands was highly valued in Israel. Paul taught Christians to work (1 Thess. 4:11; 2 Thess. 3:10; Eph. 4:28). Many images in the Gospels come from agricultural activity. The parable of the sower and the seed is more easily understood if we take into account the practice of sowing before plowing (Mark 4:1-9). Then we can better understand why so much seed was lost. In any case, the farmer in this parable should not be judged by modern farming methods.

Harvesting was also used as a figure of speech. John the Baptist said that the coming Messiah has "his win-

nowing fork . . . in his hand, and he will clear his threshing floor and will gather his wheat into the granary; but
the chaff he will burn with unquenchable fire" (Matt.
3:12).

In ancient Israel, farmers cut the grain and hauled it
to a threshing floor. Oxen were driven over the grain to
tread on the heads and thresh them (Deut. 25:4). A later
development was to have the oxen drag over the grain
a threshing sledge of planks with sharp stone teeth set
underneath (Isa. 41:15).

Translators have a hard time deciding how to translate the word for *winnowing fork* since we do not have
such a tool in our culture. It was a wooden fork with
which the threshed grain was cast into the air. The wind
drove away the chaff, the straw fell slightly aside, and
the (heavier) grains dropped at the worker's feet (Ps.
1:4). We can still observe this scene in Africa and other
parts of the world.

A sickle was used for cutting the grain. That also
became a figure of speech for final judgment (Rev.
14:15).

There are many references to fishing. Jesus called
several of his disciples as they were casting a net into
the sea (Mark 1:16-17). People fished by casting nets
(Mark 1:16) and drawing them in with the fish (Matt.
13:47-48; Luke 5:4-6), or with hook and line (Matt.
17:27). Repeatedly Jesus made himself known at fish
meals (John 6:9; 21:9). Hence, the fish became a symbol
for the Christian faith and sometimes marked Christian
homes. The Greek word for *fish* (*ichthus*) was recognized
as an acronym for "Jesus Christ, God's Son, Savior.

We must also take the pastoral life into account.
Although Israel had a long pastoral tradition, shepherds
were not in high repute in Jesus' day. That is important
in light of the fact that Christ's birth was announced

first to lowly shepherds (Luke 2). Several of Jesus' parables mention sheep or goats.

There is the eschatological parable of the separation of the sheep from the goats (Matt. 25:31-34). It makes more sense when we know that sheep and goats were herded together during the day and separated for the night. In other words, it was an illustration that people understood well from everyday observation.

In the OT, the Lord God is the "shepherd" of his people (Gen. 48:15; Ps. 23:1; Isa. 40:11). The Lord calls the shepherd Moses with his staff to lead the Israelites out of Egypt (Exod. 3–4). God assigns tribal leaders and kings to be shepherds under him (2 Sam. 5:2; 7:7; Ps. 78:71; Isa. 44:28; Jer. 22–23; Ezek. 34). Prophets are also shepherds (Jer. 17:16).

Jesus comes as the shepherd to fulfill the OT prophecies (Ezek. 34:23; Mic. 5:2; Matt. 2:6; 9:36) and searches for the lost sheep (Luke 15:1-7). In the Gospel of John, Jesus calls himself the good shepherd. He is the door to the sheepfold. In the Near East, after the sheep were in the pen for the night, the shepherd would sometimes sleep in the opening and be the gate. Jesus knows his sheep by name. He longs that there would be one flock and one shepherd (John 10:7-16).

The followers of Jesus are called God's "little flock" (Luke 12:32; cf. Rev. 7:17). Pastors are shepherds under "the chief shepherd," Jesus Christ, and care for the church as a flock (Acts 20:28-29; Heb. 13:20; 1 Pet. 5:1-4).

It is also helpful to know something about the monetary system in the days of Jesus and the apostles. Coins were in use long before Christ, and in his day Roman, Tyrian, and Jewish coins were in circulation. Exchanging currency was big business in Palestine, especially during the great festivals, when Jews came from all parts of the empire with different currency.

Tyrian coinage was preferred in offerings, so money changers did brisk business at the temple (John 2:14). The NT mentions a variety of coins, using both Greek and Latin names. There are references in the NT to hiding money in the ground. We see this in the parable of the treasure in the field (Matt. 13:44), and that of the talents (25:18-30). The latter parable also refers to banking (v. 27).

Some knowledge of the tax system in Roman times also helps us understand the NT better. One of Jesus' disciples was a former tax collector (Matt. 10:3). Readers can better understand the parable of the Pharisee and the tax collector by recognizing that tax collectors were seen as the dregs of society, collaborating with the foreign oppressors (Romans) and cheating citizens (Luke 19:8).

The Pharisees, on the other hand, flaunted their religious piety. In a parable (Luke 18:9-14), the bad man is justified and the "good" man not—the exact opposite of what Jewish hearers would have expected. It opens up the profound mysteries of God's grace, which embraces the worst of sinners.

Another aspect of the material culture of NT times is travel. In Palestine, people normally walked; a few rode. In the missionary activity of Paul, the famous Roman roads played an important role. One of the most popular ways of traveling greater distances was by ship. Information on the Roman road system and navigation by sea can be gleaned easily from Bible dictionaries.

Inns also are mentioned in the NT. We think of the birth of Jesus, when no room was found in the inn (Luke 2:7), or the parable of the good Samaritan, who took the wounded man to an inn (10:34-35).

A knowledge of products in a given culture helps us understand the NT. Christ, in his letter to the church of

Laodicea (Rev. 3:14-22), advises the church to buy gold so that they might become rich. Laodicea was known for its wealth. The readers are urged to buy white clothes, to cover up their nakedness. Laodicea was famous for its production of good cloth.

The letter suggests that the church buy eye salve. Laodicea was known for producing medication for eye diseases. The Lord wishes that Laodicea were either hot or cold. This is an allusion to Laodicea's water supply. Water had to be piped into the city from a distance, and by the time it reached Laodicea, it was no longer hot or cold. This is just one illustration of how acquaintance with the material culture of the day helps to illuminate the biblical text.

Religious Aspects

When studying the NT, interpreters must learn to distinguish between religious practices of abiding significance for the Christian church, and those that simply belonged to the Jewish or pagan culture of the first century. The early church itself did not automatically carry over Jewish OT religious practices, even though there is a continuity between the church and the old people of God. The church has not always observed that, with the founding of the church, there came a fundamental reorientation of religious life, including the worship services.

Let us look at some of the religious aspects of the culture in which the early church began and developed. At the heart of Jewish life was the synagogue. We can hardly understand the Gospels or the book of Acts without some knowledge of meetings in the Jewish synagogue. Both Jesus and the apostles initially taught in synagogues. Here the Jews read the Scriptures, prayed, sang hymns or psalms, listened to exhortations, discussed interpretations, confessed their faith, and collected money for the poor (Luke 4:16-30; Acts 13:14-41).

At the time of Jesus, the synagogue was under the influence of the Pharisees. Synagogues were found, not only in Palestine but also in the Diaspora (Jews dispersed in other nations), where they often became the springboard for Paul and his associates to establish churches. Many Jews and Greek God-fearers were converted through Paul's preaching in the synagogues.

It is important that Bible readers also know the difference between the Pharisees, the Sadducees (Acts 23:8), and the Essenes, some of whom lived at the Qumran community near the Dead Sea. A good Bible dictionary can supply such information.

Many controversies in the life of Jesus were sparked by his view of the Jewish Sabbath. If we are to understand Jesus' approach to the Sabbath, we need to inform ourselves on the Jewish Sabbath laws.

The religious festivals also played a strong role in Jesus' life. Several times Jesus went up to Jerusalem for festivals: Tabernacles, Weeks/Pentecost, Passover (Lev. 23:3-8), and even the feast of Dedication/Hanukkah (John 10:22; 1 Macc. 4:52-59). We can better understand Luke's account of the first Christian Pentecost (Acts 2) if we are familiar with the OT (Lev. 23:15-21); Jewish tradition held that the Law was given on that day.

We can hardly understand parts of the NT if we are not familiar with the temple and the city of Jerusalem. From the time of David, when he made Jerusalem his capital, up to the last chapters of the book of Revelation, Jerusalem plays a central role in the history of salvation. The temple cannot be divorced from the sacrificial system, the priesthood, and even the Sanhedrin, the chief council of the Jewish nation. For these matters, consult a Bible dictionary.

Social Dimensions

Familiarity with Jewish family life helps in our understanding of the NT. Engagements, weddings, divorce, parents, children, etc., all play roles in the biblical texts. The accounts of Jesus' birth become much clearer if we understand the significance of betrothal in Jewish society in the first century (Matt. 1:18-25).

We can hardly make sense out of the parable of the ten maidens without being familiar with Jewish wedding customs (Matt. 25:1-13). That doesn't mean that Christians must now imitate the cultural patterns of the ancient world; marriage practices vary from culture to culture, as does family life in general.

Several times both Peter and Paul exhort their Christian readers to greet one another with the holy kiss (1 Pet. 5:14; 1 Thess. 5:26). That was a Jewish social custom. Since the church emerged within a Jewish culture, early Christians carried this custom over. However, as the Gospel made inroads into societies where this was not the normal form of greeting, this practice was often dropped. It is important that believers greet each other warmly as brothers and sisters in Christ, but the form of the greeting may vary.

Eating and drinking are some of the social dimensions of life in apostolic times. Eating together was an expression of fellowship, of covenant. At formal meals people lay on divans, as Jesus and his disciples did at the Last Supper. Certainly that was also the case when Mary anointed Jesus' feet (John 12:1-8).

In the parable of the rich man and Lazarus, there is a reference to what fell from the table (Luke 16:21). This is not a commentary on the sloppy eating habits of the rich man; it probably refers to crusts on which people wiped their fingers, as we use napkins.

In a Jewish family, supper began with the breaking of

bread by the father. In imitation of this practice, a Christian group in the nineteenth century came to be known as the "bread breakers." They literally broke bread instead of using knives for slicing it. But we are not obligated to carry over Jewish social customs, just because Jesus and the apostles observed them.

Hospitality was another aspect of culture for which Jews and Near Easterners were known. The host provided the dusty traveling guest with a basin of water and a servant to wash his feet (John 13:3-17). The host would greet the guest with a kiss and perhaps even anoint his head with oil. All these things were neglected by Simon the Pharisee when he invited Jesus to his house (Luke 7:44-46).

When Jesus washed his disciples' feet, he wanted to demonstrate what it means to serve one another in humility (John 13:12-17). Some churches take literally Jesus' command to wash one another's feet (13:14-17), as a sign of serving and of daily cleansing (13:10). Others regard this as a time-bound custom that does not need to be carried over into North American worship services. In either case, believers need to learn to serve as Jesus did and to be cleansed through Jesus every day.

Likewise, the way people dressed in Jesus' day is not necessarily a pattern for believers today. If men today wear trousers, they are not violating a biblical practice, even though in Jesus' world, men did not wear trousers.

In the Greco-Roman world, especially in the East, women evidently wore a kerchief on their heads when they went to the market, for example. Paul exhorts Christian women to do the same when they gather for worship (1 Cor. 11:1-16). In other words, they were to observe the laws of propriety in their culture unless doing so would violate obedience to God (Dan. 1; Acts 5:27-29). That remains a permanent principle, but it will be expressed differently in the various cultures of our day.

What does it mean for someone to untie the thong of another person's sandal (Mark 1:7)? To gird your loins (1 Kings 18:46; 1 Pet. 1:13, KJV)? Why did Paul and Peter both forbid women to braid their hair (1 Tim. 2:9; 1 Pet. 3:3)? Surely they were not introducing a Christian hair-style. We can understand such a prohibition better if we have some knowledge of the extravagant braiding of hair in wealthy pagan circles.

The language of the NT reflects slavery, an evil social practice of the ancient Near East, the Greco-Roman world, and later centuries. Paul calls himself and his co-workers slaves of Jesus Christ (Phil. 1:1, NRSV note). When he tells the Corinthians that they have been bought with a price (1 Cor. 6:20), he's likely referring to the practice of sacred manumission, release from slavery. In several letters, Paul instructs masters and slaves on how they as Christians should relate to one another (1 Cor. 7:21-24; Col. 3:22—4:1; Eph. 6:5-9; Philem.; Swartley, 1983).

The Political World

From the first book of the Bible to the last, the biblical writings reflect a variety of political situations. We can understand these books much better if we gain some knowledge of what was going on in the world around the authors. The story of the patriarchs began in the Mesopotamia, then moved to Canaan, and finally to Egypt.

After the Exodus and the sojourn in the wilderness, Israel progressively conquered Canaanite nations and settled in the land of Canaan. For hundreds of years, Israel had to contend, not only with pockets of resistance within the land (such as the Philistines), but also with surrounding city-states, such as Damascus.

Under Saul and David, the monarchy was established. As a result, some of the great messianic promises are couched in terms of David's royal line. But the unified reign broke up after Solomon, leading to the period of the divided monarchy. It is hard to understand the prophets if we do not know whether they were speaking to the Northern Kingdom, to Judah, or to both.

The Northern Kingdom succumbed to the Assyrian onslaught in 722 B.C. Eventually, however, the Babylonians became the overlords of the Near East and made an end of the kingdom of Judah (586 B.C.). Babylon in turn was defeated by the Persians; under Cyrus some Jewish exiles were allowed to return to Judea.

Although most of the Jews remained in Mesopotamia, one group returned, rebuilt the temple, reestablished its worship practices, and gave more attention to God's law. Aramaic by then had become the everyday language of the Jews, spoken also by Jesus and the apostles.

Under the onslaught of Alexander's armies, the mighty Persian empire collapsed and Greek culture was spread over the whole Mediterranean world. Jews in the Diaspora, like their neighbors, spoke Hellenistic (not classical) Greek. By the third century B.C., Alexandrian Jews began to translate the Hebrew Scriptures into that Koiné (common) Greek, in the Septuagint version. In the first century A.D., the NT books, mostly by Jewish writers, were also written in Greek, the language of the Mediterranean world.

With the death of Alexander (323 B.C.), his empire broke up. Judea was caught between the Syrian Seleucid rulers and the Ptolemies of Egypt. Both tried at various times to gain control over Judea. Antiochus Epiphanes, king of Syria in the second century B.C., tried to stamp out the Jewish religion. This led to the Maccabean wars and a brief period of Jewish independence.

However, Rome was on the march, and by 63 B.C. the Romans took over Palestine. All the books of the NT were written while the Romans ruled the known world.

Herod the Great ruled over the Jews by the grace of the Romans. He engaged in colossal building operations, including the reconstruction of the Jerusalem temple (John 2:20). The Sanhedrin (council and court of 70 plus the high priest) monitored the religious life of the Jews and cooperated with the Roman authorities. Our Lord was born several years before the end of Herod the Great's reign early in 4 B.C. (Matt. 2). When Herod died, the country was parceled out to three of his sons.

Jesus grew up in Galilee, under the reign of Herod Antipas. Archelaus ruled over Samaria, Judea, and Idumea. Because of his misrule, the Romans deposed him and sent in a governor who had his seat in Caesarea, on the coast. The governor best known to Bible readers was Pilate, who condemned our Lord to death. Herod Agrippa persecuted the church, then died (Acts 12). Paul was imprisoned in Caesarea under Felix, saw King Agrippa II, and was sent to Rome under Festus in about 60 (Acts 21ff.). Decades of unrest and the destruction of Jerusalem (70) led to direct Roman rule.

When Jesus was born, Caesar Augustus was on the Roman throne (from 27 B.C.; Luke 2:1). He was the adopted son of Julius Caesar. In the reign of his successor, Tiberias (A.D. 14-37), John the Baptist began his ministry (Luke 3:1), and Jesus was crucified. Tiberias was succeeded by Gaius Caligula (37-41), who does not appear in the NT.

Acts 11:28 mentions his successor, Claudius (41-54), who ordered the Jews out of Rome. That brought Aquila and Priscilla to Paul at Corinth in about 51, when Gallio was proconsul of Achaia (Acts 18:2, 12). When Paul appealed to Caesar (Acts 25), Nero had already ascended the throne (54-68). After the fire of Rome (64), Christians were persecuted by Nero; both Paul and Peter apparently lost their lives under his rule. Likely the apostle John had Nero in mind when he spoke of the beast that persecutes the saints (Rev. 13:1-8).

After three emperors ruled for a brief time in 69, Vespasian became emperor (69-79). His son, Titus, led the Roman forces in the destruction of Jerusalem (66-70) and later became emperor (79-81). Near the end of the first century, Domitian was emperor (81-96). Likely Revelation was written during his reign.

Wherever the early missionaries took the gospel and the first-century church was found, believers encountered the Roman authorities, Roman soldiers, and Roman law. Hence, it is rather important to be familiar with the political situations in which the apostles found themselves as they wrote the books of the NT.

The Word of God has come to us clothed in the dress of the ancient world. We are not obligated to carry over many of the specific material, religious, social, or political aspects of ancient oriental societies. They were the staging on which the drama of salvation history was portrayed. The church needs to exercise careful discernment on these matters.

The hermeneutical task of modern interpreters of the Bible is like that of a carpenter if the carpenter works with meters and centimeters but is given the measurements in yards and feet. We must constantly transmute one into the other to get it right. The message of the Bible is applicable to every age and culture, but it has to be recast and put into suitable forms.

In another analogy, most people in our day have

more than one set of clothing. We have work clothes, sports clothes, formal dress, Sunday clothes, and sleep-wear. Some countries even have a national dress, such as the dirndl in Austria or the sari in India. One person may wear different clothes for different occasions. The clothes differ, but the person is the same.

So it is with the Word of God: the message is the same for every culture and for all ages. But the dress in which it has come to us may not always be the same as the dress it dons today in different countries and cultures.

10

OT Literary Genres

*T*he 39 books of the OT represent a variety of literary genres. A literary genre is a group of texts with similar characteristics, making a recognizable type of writing. About 40 percent of the OT is in narrative form. But we also have poetic books and wisdom literature. Such genres can be found among the literature of Israel's neighbors as well.

Prophecy is an activity and a type of literature that appears in various nations of the ancient Near East. Yet the character of prophecy in Israel is unique. It is inspired by the Lord God.

In our interpretation of the Scriptures, it is important to recognize that poems, proverbs, narratives, and prophecy cannot be treated in exactly the same way.

The books of the OT are classified in different ways in our English Bibles. In the Hebrew Bible, the five books of Moses are called the Law (*Torah*). This Pentateuch was always regarded as unique and basic for understanding the covenant between God and Israel.

The second division in the Hebrew canon is the Prophets (*Nebiim*), including books such as Joshua, Judges, 1 and 2 Samuel, and 1 and 2 Kings.

The third division of the Hebrew Bible is called the Writings (*Kethubim*).

Some authors refer to the Hebrew Scriptures by using the initial letters of these three divisions to form an acronym, *Tanakh* (*ABD*, 6:318). No doubt a number of factors led to the threefold division of the OT books. But literary genre is hardly the only determinative principle.

Our discussion of the literary genres of the OT will not follow this threefold division of the Hebrew canon. Instead, we focus on the main types of literature found in the OT in general. In the process, we shall give some suggestions on how to handle these different literary genres in our efforts to interpret the OT.

Narrative

Since the Bible is essentially a history of salvation, almost half of the OT is in narrative form. Christianity is a historical faith; it is not simply a belief system or a religious ideology. It has its roots in historical events. Again and again God in his mercy has reached down into human history and made himself known. The biblical writers witness to those revelations.

The accounts of important events in the history of salvation are, however, not simply chronicles or reports of what happened. The authors of the biblical narratives wrote from a theological standpoint. They were not interested merely in facts, but chiefly in how the people of God fitted into God's saving purposes in human history.

This explains, in part, why books such as Joshua, Judges, Samuel, and Kings are classified as prophetic. They are not simply historical accounts; they also teach important theological truths. Even as we read them today, we are addressed, exhorted, warned, or comforted.

The Bible was written for ordinary people, and people generally find a story more absorbing than theological concepts. Biblical narratives are generally quite life-like in character and in action. Bible stories make learning easier. They enable us to enter into the lives of people who ages ago learned to walk with God. Yet they also open up the deep caverns of human wickedness. Like the parable stories of Jesus, OT narratives teach profound theological truths implicitly. Without spelling everything out, they hit their mark.

Christian readers sometimes ask why certain seamy stories were included in sacred literature. Why, for example, is that embarrassing story of Judah and Tamar recorded? The answer is given right in the narrative (Gen. 38); Perez was the ancestor of David (38:29; Ruth 4:18-22). The NT adds, "It is evident that our Lord came from Judah" (Heb. 7:14).

Why is the story of David and Bathsheba included in the Scriptures? Again, our Lord was a descendant of David. The story clearly shows that salvation is by grace, a grace that forgives and restores. It powerfully teaches us the potential for wickedness that lurks in the human heart. The story was certainly not told as encouragement for us to imitate David. Instead, it warns us not to enter the path that leads to adultery and murder.

Sometimes people ask, Why would a book like Judges, with its accounts of Israel's moral decay, be included in the Bible? This book teaches us valuable lessons. Not only does it underscore again that salvation is by grace alone. It also shows us what happens to a society in which people do what is right in their own eyes.

Although narrative dominates the OT, the so-called historical books contain much more than biblical stories. Embedded in the narrative sections of the OT are a great many other literary genres. We have proverbs (as in

1 Sam. 10:12), riddles (Judg. 14:14), and fables (Judg. 9:8-15; 2 Kings 14:9). Nathan's parable brought king David to his knees and provides a striking climax to David's dastardly treatment of Bathsheba and her husband (2 Sam. 12:1-4).

The narrator will also include songs (as in Num. 21:17-18). The genealogies incorporated in the narrative sections make rather boring reading for us, but they were quite significant in the life of Israel.

There is also much legal material in the narratives of the OT. Laws are so prominent in the Pentateuch that the five books of Moses are simply called the Law (*Torah*) in the Hebrew Bible. Within the collections of laws are different types.

There is, for example, casuistic or case law: if a certain situation arises, then this is the penalty. But there are also apodictic laws, giving unconditional and absolute commands, as found in the Ten Commandments. In addition, we have rules governing agricultural practices, family, and social life. A good part of Exodus and almost all of Leviticus gives us laws that regulate Israel's life, including such things as the dietary laws and the whole sacrificial system.

We shall say something later about how Christians today should handle these OT laws (see chap. 12). At this point we must remind ourselves that the laws God gave Israel were an expression of his love and grace. They should not be seen as a heavy yoke or as a basis for salvation. There was no salvation by works in the OT, as there is none in the NT.

Moral law was given to the people to help Israel become the kind of agent God could use in bringing the light of the covenant to the nations of the world (Gen. 12:3; Isa. 49:6). The many laws governing interpersonal relations are also a gift to the people of God.

The sacrificial system was designed to make it possible for a weak and sinful people to remain in covenant with God. Prayers and sacrifices were a way of righting relations between God and his people. All of the OT laws arise out of the covenant that God established with a people, whom he had redeemed by his grace and power out of Egyptian slavery. God meant his laws to make out of Israel "a priestly kingdom and a holy nation" (Exod. 19:5-6), ready to share with the nations the knowledge of God and obedience to God.

In our attempt to interpret the narratives of the OT, we should always ask ourselves how a particular story contributes to developing God's plan of salvation for humanity. God chose Israel to be the people through whom he wanted to work out his saving plans in history. Hence, the OT narratives must always be interpreted in the context of God's covenant with Israel.

As Christians, we now read these narratives in the fuller light of God's revelation in Christ. Yet we should not overlook the many practical lessons that can be found in the narratives of the OT. That does not mean that we read back into these stories what the NT teaches and in that way try to Christianize them. We must first listen to what these stories had to say to their original readers, then see how the NT used them, and also ask ourselves, What can *we* learn from them?

Wisdom

Three books in the OT are classified as wisdom literature: Proverbs, Job, and Ecclesiastes. Israel had its wise men who through experience and observation learned much that contributed to the welfare of the people of God. They recorded these insights for posterity.

Solomon was known as a wise king and "Teacher" (Eccles. 1:1). Priests and prophets were viewed as wisdom teachers (Jer. 18:18). Peoples other than Israel also had wisdom literature. However, in the wisdom literature of the Bible, the fear of the Lord is acknowledged as the beginning of knowledge and wisdom (Prov. 1:7). In these biblical books, we are not merely offered books of human learning. Rather, we find wisdom teaching that comes out of a profound faith in God.

In Ecclesiastes we have what might be called cynical wisdom. The book is a monologue on the meaninglessness and purposelessness of life. The writer encourages his readers to enjoy life as much as they can, but to remember that, in the end, it is all like grasping the wind. Some Jewish scholars later wondered why this book had been taken into the biblical canon. Christian readers have often had similar questions.

To be sure, at first blush it appears that the writer of Ecclesiastes has gone through life without faith in God. He compares humans to animals: "For the fate of humans and the fate of animals is the same, as one dies, so dies the other" (3:19). This verse is misused by Jehovah's Witnesses to support their teaching that evil persons do not continue to exist after death.

At the end of the book, the Teacher does witness to his true faith in God. He admonishes his readers to remember their creator in the days of their youth (Eccles. 12:1). In closing, he exhorts, "Fear God, and keep his commandments" (12:13). Evidently the author wants to show the emptiness of life here on earth when people try to live without God. Seen from that vantage point, Ecclesiastes carries a powerful message for our day.

The book of Job is different but also belongs to wisdom literature. Although it opens and closes with a brief narrative passage, it is mainly a disputation. Job and his three friends debate the question of Job's suffering. Job defends his innocence, and his friends argue that, on the basis of the law of retribution, he must be guilty, and God is punishing him for his sin.

Both Job and his friends say things that are patently wrong, but in the end Job is justified. The book shows in a powerful way that, when individuals suffer, they are not necessarily being punished for their own sins. Job was an innocent sufferer. But he had to learn to bow humbly to God's mysterious ways and not rail against God when he couldn't find the reason for his suffering.

The book of Proverbs is different from the other two wisdom books. Its wisdom is taught in proverbs, concise statements of truths learned from human experience. Godly people have gone through life and have learned through observation what contributes to a wholesome life and what harms it.

The opposite of such wisdom is foolishness, seen in unfaithfulness, laziness, sexual promiscuity, lawlessness, and so forth. Wisdom, by contrast, manifests itself in respect for elders, helping the poor, moderation in food and drink, family loyalty, and the like. Proverbial sayings are a teaching method; they help to engrave these truths on the minds of the young.

Proverbs teach not absolute but probable truths. They offer general principles for successful living and do not spell out exceptions. They are not mechanical formulas, but they do suggest procedures to follow. To see them as commandments or even promises is to use them in a way the writers did not intend.

A number of the proverbs express opposite points of view. Hence, a single proverb cannot be held up as if it were a divine law. For example, the writer exhorts the reader not to "answer fools according to their folly" (Prov. 26:4). Then the next verse says the opposite: "Answer fools according to their folly" (cf. CTV: "If you answer any fools, show how foolish they are").

Take the matter of bribes. On one hand, they lead to prosperity (17:8); on the other hand, they tend to pervert justice (17:23). By placing these opposites close to each other, the writers are probably suggesting that we must use discrimination when applying them.

The law of retribution, noticed in the book of Job, is in evidence also in Proverbs. The godly are promised that their "house" (family) will endure (12:7) and that people will be blessed by remembering them (10:7). On the other hand, "the house of the wicked is destroyed" (14:11). Yet, as in the case of Job, the exact opposite sometimes happens, and so we must not formulate a dogma on the basis of a single proverb. A proverb often expresses only a narrow slice of reality.

In applying such proverbs to our Christian life, we must take their genre into account. We read a comforting proverb: "Commit your work to the Lord, and your plans will be established" (16:3). This is not a guarantee that every plan we lay before the Lord will succeed.

One proverb says, "Those who listen to me will be secure and will live at ease, without dread of disaster" (1:33). That would be cold comfort for believers who live in societies where they are persecuted for their faith.

Those who espouse the health-and-wealth gospel would find support in this proverb: "Honor the Lord with your substance and with the first fruits of all your produce; then your barns will be filled with plenty, and your vats will be bursting with wine" (3:9-10). But we have already seen from the book of Job that it doesn't always work that way. What shall those suffering from famine say when they read, "The Lord does not let the righteous go hungry" (10:3). Many of God's faithful people have died and are dying of hunger.

A proverb that has caused Christian parents much

pain is the one found in Proverbs 22:6: "Train children in the right way, and when old, they will not stray." Devout parents, who did their best in bringing up their children in the fear of the Lord, sometimes see a son or daughter become wayward and forsake the Christian faith altogether.

Yet after allowing for many exceptions, the proverbs are generally true to life and must not be shrugged off lightly. Believers do face suffering. Yet in general, where believers take seriously their requirements for happy and healthy life, they can expect the blessing of God.

The wisdom taught in Proverbs is not simply shrewdness or intelligence. Instead, it is based on a relationship with God. "In all your ways acknowledge him, and he shall direct your paths" (Prov. 3:6, KJV).

Poetry

Poetry can be found embedded in the books of the OT in narrative passages, in prophetical books, and in wisdom literature. The best-known book of Hebrew poetry is, of course, the Psalter. The Psalms are full of emotive figurative language, and that needs to be observed when we try to interpret them. Poetry cannot be read the same way we read a story or a letter.

In contrast to the prophets, through whom God speaks to the people of their day, the psalmists speak to God. Their songs and prayers have been a great help to believers all through the ages, as they tell God their joys and sorrows, their complaints and their successes, their praises and the deepest desires of their hearts.

Many types of OT poetry can be found in the Psalms. Some psalms are laments, with individual and corporate laments. Others are thanksgiving songs. These were sung in worship at the temple and played an important role in the life of God's people. The entire community had an opportunity to voice its joyful gratitude to God.

There also are hymns of praise, extolling God as Creator, Protector, or Redeemer of Israel. Several of the Psalms review the entire history of Israel and praise God for his steadfast love that he has shown to his people. There are love songs (such as Ps. 45), songs of trust, of celebration, and songs of wisdom (as in 127).

One type of psalm that has caused Christian believers considerable difficulty is the imprecatory psalm, in which the psalmist vents anger at his and God's enemies. Some of the imprecatory psalms are quite harsh (such as 137). Paul quotes a version of Psalm 4:4 in Ephesians 4:26, "Be angry but do not sin." It appears, then, that to be disgusted with evil is not in itself sin, but it would certainly be wrong to act out our anger toward other people.

It may in fact be that the psalmist, by expressing his anger in his laments to God, is kept from carrying out his wrath towards others. In any case, he identifies with God's wrath against all ungodliness.

There are also several psalms in which Israel's king is exalted. These are sometimes called royal psalms or even coronation hymns (such as 2, 72, 110). Since Christ is the greater David, who today is seated at God's right hand, we may also speak of these psalms as messianic. The NT writers often apply Psalm 110:1 to Jesus Christ being exalted to sit at God's right hand (Matt. 22:44; Acts 2:34; 1 Cor. 15:25; Eph. 1:20; Heb. 1:3, 13). The NT frequently quotes the Psalms in accounts of Christ's life and death; indeed, our Lord himself quoted the Psalms many times.

The songs and prayers of the Psalter are so true to life that they have become a constant source of spiritual nourishment for Christian believers, in their private lives as well as in corporate worship.

Prophecy

Narrative, wisdom literature, and poetry were known also among the nations surrounding Israel, and so was prophecy, as shown by recent archaeological discoveries. Yet prophecy in Israel is uniquely inspired by the Lord God experienced by Israel (*ABD*, 5:477ff.; *HCBD*, "Prophet").

For some Bible readers, the word *prophecy* suggests predictions of future events, but prophecy has more to do with "forthtelling" than "foretelling." The prophets are God's messengers who proclaim God's will to his people. They call Israel to repentance when the nation becomes apostate; they warn God's people of the dire consequences of disregarding the covenant. But they also hold out forgiveness and hope.

The prophets' messages vary, depending on the moral and spiritual conditions of their contemporaries. Occasionally they cast rays of light into the more distant future, of which they themselves are probably not fully aware. In the light of the NT, we can see the intent of such messages more clearly. For example, Joel announces a locust plague and calls it "the day of the Lord" (Joel 1–2). But this local and temporary judgment is also a telescope through which we can see the coming day of the Lord at the end of the age.

To interpret the prophets' messages correctly, we must always first ask, To whom are they speaking? Usually the nation of Israel is addressed. Yet with the division of the kingdom, we have prophets who speak to the Northern Kingdom, and others who speak to the Southern. These same prophets often speak oracles of judgment on the surrounding nations—Assyria, Babylon, Damascus, Edom, and so forth. Within Israel they address the king, the priesthood, the wealthy, the women, and others, quite specifically.

Because the prophets usually address Israel as a nation, it makes sense that their prophecies of future salvation will be given in terms of the whole people, the nation. The NT writers also speak in peoplehood terms (king, kingdom, rule, throne, nation). But the new people of God that emerges through Christ's saving work is international, composed of believers from every tongue and tribe (Rev. 7:9-10). The church is a new nation, cutting across old dividing lines (Eph. 2:13-14). It is "a chosen race, a royal priesthood, *a holy nation,* God's own people" (1 Pet. 2:9, emphasis added).

Some of the prophecies that predicted Israel's future were fulfilled when Israel returned from Babylon. Others were fulfilled with the coming of Christ. Some prophecies are being fulfilled as those saved are gathered into the church (Acts 2:16-21).

Other prophecies, such as the hope of a new heaven and a new earth (Isa. 66:22; Rev. 21:1), will be fulfilled in God's own time, in the future. Some of this may already be starting with the church, as believers are redeemed, reign on the earth (Rev. 5:9-10), and are being transformed into the image of Christ, who is the truest image of God (2 Cor. 3:18; 4:4-6, 16-17).

The style of the prophetic messages is unique. Often the prophet introduces a topic and then comes at it again and again from different angles. Occasionally he breaks into poetry; the language of the prophets is rich in figures of speech. Prophets make use of customary imagery. When, for example, Isaiah foresees the day when the sun will be darkened and the moon will refuse to shine, he is not necessarily speaking of the end of the world (Isa. 13:9-11). He uses cosmic imagery to describe the destruction of Babylon.

Sometimes the coming age is described in earthly terms: the wolf lives with the lamb, the leopard with the goat, the calf with the lion, the child plays near the hole of the cobra (Isa. 11:6-9). But in Isaiah 35:8-10, the prophet predicts that when God will redeem his people, there will be no wild beasts in the way. Clearly, then, the description of the messianic age in chapters 11 and 35 must be understood figuratively. It need not be a description of a future earthly millennium but of the coming age of salvation.

NT writers understood the picture language of the OT. In describing the ministry of John the Baptist, Luke (3:4-6) quotes Isaiah 40:3-5 as describing the moral and spiritual renewal coming with God's salvation. "Every valley shall be filled, and every mountain and hill shall be made low, and the crooked shall be made straight, and the rough ways made smooth." Luke didn't think John's ministry called for geographical or topographical changes. Isaiah was describing Israel's return from Babylon in vivid pictorial language; it was reapplied by John.

In our interpretation of the prophetic books, we should avoid constantly looking for their fulfillment in current events. For example, we cannot carry over the promises given to ancient Israel willy-nilly to the modern state of Israel. I was a seminary student soon after World War II and found a book with the title *Japan in the Light of Prophecy*. It was written before the war, I read it after the war, and all the predictions about Japan turned out to be wrong.

This was a healthy warning to me not to seek specific fulfillment of OT prophecies in current events. Those who hold the Bible in one hand and the newspaper in the other, for purposes of cross-referencing the two on predictive details, contribute little to the life of the church. They fail to hear what God is really saying to them through the prophets.

Some parts of the prophetic books are hard to understand. Yet there is an amazing amount of material in these writings that profoundly rewards devotional reading and supports challenging exhortation today. This, of course, calls for a transposition of these prophetic messages from their original intent to our life in today's world.

11

NT Literary Genres

*T*here are different types of literature in the NT, just as there are in the OT. Several genres found in the NT were well-known in the world in which the apostolic writers lived. Narrative literature was common enough, as was letter writing. In the Jewish world, apocalyptic was a recognized genre of literature.

There is, however, one type of literature that, according to many scholars, came into being through the emergence of the Christian church: Gospel writing. The coming of Jesus, his life and teaching and, above all, his death and resurrection, seemed to call for a genre of literature for which it is difficult to identify precedents.

Later, many apocryphal Gospels were written in poor imitation of our canonical Gospels, and usually they are not narratives.

We want to say a few things about our Gospels in general and then focus on several types of literature in the rest of the NT.

Gospels

The Gospels in General. The word *gospel* (*euangelion*) was a well-known word in apostolic times. It was not a religious word to begin with. Literally, the word means "good news" or "glad message." In the Greek-speaking world, the word was used to designate any joyous message. Even the decrees of Caesar were called *euangelia*, and Caesar's birthday was an *euangelion* for the whole world.

The Greek version of the OT used the verb (*euangelizomai*) from the same root, to announce the good news of Israel's redemption from the exile (Isa. 40:9; 52:7; 61:1). In Luke 4:18-19, Jesus applies the words of Isaiah 61:1-2 to his own ministry, "to bring good news" to the poor (with the same verb).

The NT writers have taken over the noun *gospel, good news,* from the general or political sphere and used it for the good news of salvation in Christ. Paul uses the word *euangelion* twenty-three times in an absolute sense, without defining it. The verb *euangelizomai* refers to the proclamation of the joyous news of Christ's death and resurrection, by which he offers us forgiveness of sins and the gift of eternal life.

When the word *euangelion* was co-opted by NT writers to designate the good news of salvation, it referred to spoken, proclaimed good news. Eventually this oral proclamation was written down, and the books that contained the good news were called Gospels.

How many authors undertook to write Gospels is not known; Luke suggests that there were a number of them (Luke 1:1-2). We have four canonical Gospels. In terms of chronology, the letters of the NT preceded the Gospels. But since the Gospels tell of the birth, ministry, and death of our Lord Jesus, it is appropriate that they should stand first in our NT canon.

Our Gospels are actually anonymous. Early tradition, however, has ascribed them to Matthew, Mark, Luke, and John. It is widely held that Mark was the earliest Gospel, and that the first line in his Gospel, "The beginning of the gospel (*euaggelion*) of Jesus Christ" (1:1, KJV), served as the title of the book.

As other Gospels were written, they came to be distinguished from each another by the names of the traditional authors: *Kata Matthaion* (according to Matthew), *Kata Markon*, *Kata Lukan*, and *Kata Ioannen*.

Christian readers have found the Gospels to be the most attractive of the books of the Bible. Far more Gospel manuscripts have been preserved than those of other books of the NT. That shouldn't surprise us, for without the Gospels, the NT canon would have no foundation. The Gospels explain the mission of the church's Founder, Jesus Christ.

Attempts have been made to identify our Gospels with some known type of literature, but with difficulty. Many scholars have thought that the Gospels represent a unique genre. We can hardly say that they are biographies, even though they do provide us with some biographical information.

Would a biographer write the story of a person's life and skip the first thirty years? That's what we have in our Gospels. After an account of Christ's birth (in two Gospels), they describe approximately three years of his public ministry, and then concentrate on his death and resurrection.

We could perhaps classify the Gospels more broadly as narrative literature, for there is a great deal of narrative in our Gospels. Like biography, history writing was a well-known art in NT times. But our Gospels have a great many discourses alongside narrative sections.

Within narrative literature, the Gospels may be regarded as a subgenre of "laudatory biography," for which examples are claimed in other writers. Some students compare the Gospels with the OT prophets when they give a biography showing "the suffering of a righteous person." This is a model of faithfulness to be imitated (*ABD*, 2:1078-9).

In any case, the canonical Gospels were written, as stated in John's Gospel, to lead people to faith and life in Jesus Christ (John 20:31). Jesus brought the new wine of the kingdom, and that called for new wineskins. Hence, a Gospel literature developed, under the guidance of the Holy Spirit.

Our Gospels have come to us in (common) Greek, but the everyday language of our Lord and his apostles was Aramaic. This means that behind our Greek Gospels there is an Aramaic (at least oral) tradition that has an effect on both the Greek style and the meaning of words and idioms.

Even so, our Gospels are not identical in style. Each Gospel writer expresses himself in his own unique way and leaves the stamp of his individual personality on his writing. Besides, the Gospels have different audiences in mind, and their authors emphasize somewhat different theological and social themes. They select their material and order it in different ways, even though the overall framework of the life of Jesus is similar.

Within this framework, the Fourth Gospel goes a somewhat independent path. The other three are called the "synoptic Gospels" (because they "see together"). Matthew and Luke largely follow the narrative path recorded by Mark but insert extra material. They never agree with each other in the order of events when they depart from Mark's sequence.

This is not the place to discuss thoroughly the complex interrelationship of these three Gospels. About 90 percent of Mark can be found in Matthew. Matthew has much in common with Luke, but it includes material not found in Mark or in Luke. Luke has about 50 percent of Mark. Besides what Luke has in common with Matthew, it also has a considerable amount of unique material.

The units that Matthew and Luke have in common and that are not in Mark are often called Q for *Quelle* (German: source). This is a supposed common source reconstructed from the two Gospels (but never independently seen).

For interpreters, it would have been much simpler if we had only one Gospel. If our Gospels were histories only, one might have been enough. But the good news of salvation can be proclaimed in many different ways, to various audiences in various life situations. We would be much poorer if we had only one Gospel.

In the second century, Tatian, a Christian apologist from Assyria, spliced our four Gospels together. This first harmony of the Gospels is called the Diatessaron ("through four"). It became so popular that it was translated into many languages and was used by the Syriac church into the fifth century.

Also in the second century, Marcion from Pontus created a canon without the OT and with Luke as the only Gospel (edited to reduce Jewish elements) and ten of Paul's letters. Marcion was excommunicated and counted as a heretic. His rejection of three Gospels helped the church see how important it was to distinguish between true and spurious works and to make its own canon. In the long run, neither Marcion's canon nor Tatian's Diatessaron could dislodge the fourfold Gospels.

In our attempts to interpret the Gospels, we should always remember that they were written a whole generation after Jesus was exalted into glory. For an entire generation, the Gospel material was transmitted orally. Eventually this oral tradition was recorded by Matthew and John, members of the Twelve; by Mark, an associate of the apostle Peter; and by Luke, a non-Jew who was Paul's companion (Luke may have joined Paul at Troas; the first "we" passage begins at Acts 16:10).

Because the Gospels were written so much later than the events of Jesus' ministry, the context of his original words and actions was no longer that of the writers. Moreover, our Evangelists had different audiences in mind from those to whom Jesus first addressed his message of the kingdom of God.

For example, the parable of the lost sheep in Luke 15 stresses God's love for lost sinners. That same parable in Matthew 18 speaks of the pastoral care that Christ's followers are to offer to "these little ones."

Jesus spoke Aramaic, but we have his teachings in Greek. Hence, his message was recast to fit the different language and culture.

If we are to grasp the message of Jesus, we must have a correct understanding of his fundamental theme: *the kingdom of God* (or, as in Matthew, the kingdom of heaven). By the coming of Jesus, the kingdom of God has broken into this world in a new way.

The word *kingdom* refers to God's reign. The term must not be understood in some geographical or nationalistic sense. Jesus did not come to establish a political realm like the kingdoms of this world (John 18:36). Instead, Jesus was establishing the rule of God over the hearts and lives of people who acknowledge him as Lord and King. Thereby he was creating a new people of God.

The miracles of Jesus are signs of the inbreaking of the kingdom. Jesus' parables illustrate different aspects of the reign of God. The kingdom that he established, as he explains to Pilate, "is not from this world" (John 18:36-37). The source of its peaceful and redeeming character is God.

The reign of God established by Jesus is a present reality. But there is also a future dimension to this reign, which is not yet visible, the eternal kingdom of God. In several parables, Jesus speaks of that eternal kingdom in the age to come. We might mention the parable of the sheep and the goats (Matt. 25). At the Last Supper, Jesus says that he will not again drink of the fruit of the vine "until that day when I drink it new in the kingdom of God" (Mark 14:25).

Embedded in the Gospels are several different literary genres, most of which we cannot discuss at this point. We find proverbs, dialogues, and narrative, including a long passion story. We limit ourselves to the Sermon on the Mount and the parables of Jesus.

The Sermon on the Mount. Probably no part of the Gospels has made such an impact on Bible readers as the Sermon on the Mount (Matt. 5–7). People who do not remember the entire sermon may still know of the Beatitudes or the Lord's Prayer.

Matthew gives us the Sermon in longer form than does Luke in the Sermon on the Plain (Luke 6:17-49). In both accounts Jesus teaches regarding the life of his followers who have accepted the reign of God and entered his kingdom.

Obviously, these teachings of Jesus are not for unbelievers; they are designed for all believers and not just a select group of them. The Sermon is a summary of the ethical teachings of Jesus, primarily for all of his disciples, yet with some awareness of the crowds listening (Matt. 5:1; Luke 7:1). Over the years, there have been many attempts to tone down Jesus' demands in the Sermon.

In the Middle Ages, a popular view of the Sermon was that the more stringent demands in the teachings of Jesus were to be observed by those who had spiritual vocations (such as priests, bishops, nuns); the less demanding were for ordinary believers. But there are no grounds for making such a distinction.

At the time of the Reformation, the Sermon on the Mount was not generally taken very seriously either in Roman Catholic or Protestant circles. By contrast, the Anabaptists held that the teachings of Jesus in the Sermon were binding on all those who confessed Christ's name, including Jesus' teaching of nonresistance (Matt. 5:38-48).

Martin Luther developed his two-kingdom theology. In it, the Sermon was to be taken seriously in a believer's personal life. But when it came to public office (serving as magistrate, soldier, etc.), a Christian followed the laws of the kingdom of this world.

Lutheran Orthodoxy generally held that the Sermon on the Mount posed an unattainable ethical ideal. They supposed that it was designed to drive people to despair of their own ability to measure up to God's standards, and thus lead to repentance. It was a *praeparatio evangelica* (preparation for the gospel). In the words of Paul, the "law was a disciplinarian until Christ came" (Gal. 3:25, author's trans.).

In the seventeenth century, Pietists in the Lutheran Church reacted against this interpretation. The founder of Pietism, Philip Spener from Alsace, emphasized holiness of life. That meant that in everyday life, every believer was supposed to follow the teachings of Jesus in the Sermon.

In liberal theology, the Sermon on the Mount was often described as attitudinal ethics. The kingdom of God was understood as something inward, and the Sermon had to do with people's attitudes. Surely Jesus would not have wanted to lay a heavy yoke on his followers by demanding of them that they actually obey the teachings of the Sermon! Jesus only expected people to develop right attitudes, they claimed.

In the teachings of the nineteenth-century Englishman John Darby, as popularized by C. I. Scofield in his *Reference Bible* (first edition, 1909), the Sermon on the Mount played no great role. Scofield claimed that Jesus wanted to restore the political kingdom to Israel, and since Israel rejected its king (Jesus), the kingdom was postponed. The ethical laws of the Sermon on the Mount were given to govern the future millennial kingdom. Since that kingdom has not yet been realized, the teachings of Jesus in the Sermon will be applicable much later, in the millennium, after Israel has been restored, said Scofield.

There have been other attempts at interpreting the Sermon on the Mount. Leo Tolstoy, a Russian living a century ago, came to a radical understanding of the Sermon. If applied to society as a whole, it would do away with oaths, with courts, with police, with wars, and so forth. But given the state of sinful humanity, such a goal would obviously not be achieved.

Early in the twentieth century, Albert Schweitzer was influenced by a German NT professor named Johannes Weiss. Schweitzer held that Jesus expected the inbreaking of the eternal kingdom in his lifetime. Jesus even went to his death in the hope that he could accelerate its coming. Schweitzer taught that Jesus expected the "interim ethics" of his Sermon to be taken seriously in the short time until the dawning of the eternal kingdom. Since, however, the present age did not end, the Sermon has little relevance for us, according to Schweitzer.

We see, then, that interpretations of the Sermon on the Mount are determined largely by how we understand the concept of the kingdom of God. If we believe that Jesus brought the kingdom of God, and we are now members of his kingdom, then the teachings of Jesus must be taken seriously by all believers.

It is obvious that God's people often fail in living up

to these standards. But with the help of the Spirit of God, they are enabled to become more and more Christlike, as they seek to embody in everyday life the teachings of Jesus in the Sermon.

The Parables. The parables of Jesus belong to the better known parts of the Gospels. Even people who do not profess to be Christians are familiar with at least some of them. The language of the parables has penetrated our everyday speech. Even unbelievers speak of being a good Samaritan, of not burying our talents, of counting the cost, and so forth.

At first blush, the parables seem easy to understand. But when we try to apply them to life in the twentieth century, the matter becomes more complicated. Yet they continue to fascinate Bible readers, and new books on the parables are published annually.

Definition of Parable. Sometimes it is said quite simply that parables are earthly stories with heavenly meanings. Although there is some truth in such a statement, it will hardly do as a definition of the genre *parable*. The Greek word *parabolē* means something that is put or thrown at the side as an analogy or illustration. The word occurs forty-eight times in the Synoptics and twice in the epistle to the Hebrews.

However, to understand how the Greek word is used, we must look at the Hebrew word standing behind it. The Hebrew *mashal*, translated "parable," has a much wider meaning. It includes proverbs, riddles, fables, allegories, illustrations, and so forth. Although the NT authors write in Greek, they think like Hebrews, and so the Greek word *parabolē* must be understood as having a much wider field of application.

A parable story must not be confused with narrative, for it does not describe a historical event, though sometimes the story concept may come from one. A parable is a literary creation of Jesus. Hence, we needn't ask, for example, who took care of the ninety-nine while the shepherd looked for the one lost sheep (Luke 15). The parable has its setting in Palestinian life and underscores God's love in seeking the lost, as this was reflected in Jesus extending God's grace to sinners.

We have about thirty parables in the Gospels that have the word *parable* in them. Seventeen parables are not called parables, yet they are parables. There also are a host of parabolic sayings not in story form. For example, Jesus instructs his disciples to be wise as serpents and innocent as doves (Matt. 10:16). Here we have a parable or comparisons that are similes. It is estimated that, when all this is added together, about one-third of all the sayings of Jesus are in parable form.

Some people ask, Why does the Gospel of John have no parables? It is true there are no parable stories in John. However, there are many parabolic sayings. We have a parable when Jesus tells Nicodemus, "The wind blows where it chooses, and you hear the sound of it, but you do not know where it comes from or where it goes. So it is with everyone who is born of the Spirit" (3:8).

The Interpretation of Parables. In the early centuries of Christianity, there was a tendency to interpret the parables allegorically. Allegory was popular in Alexandrian Judaism, and Christians borrowed this method from the Jewish community.

Origen of Alexandria interpreted the parable of the good Samaritan like this: The man who went down to Jericho is Adam. Jerusalem is paradise. Jericho is the world. The robbers are the enemies of humanity. The wounds of the victim are our sins. The priest who passed by is the law. The Levite represents the prophets. The two denarii are the knowledge of the Father and the

Son. The innkeeper stands for the angels, who watch over the church. The promise to return is Christ's parousia.

This kind of interpretation remained popular throughout the Middle Ages. But, as apparent, we cannot recover the message of the parable in this way. We might admire the imagination of the interpreter, but it is a completely arbitrary approach.

At the time of the Reformation in the sixteenth century, Luther and Calvin condemned this allegorical interpretation of the parables. The details of a parabolic story are not meant to be interpreted, they said; they are simply the staging, the backdrop. The interpreter has to discover the major thrust of the parable. In spite of these denunciations of allegorizing interpretation, it never really died out.

A century ago, Adolf Jülicher, a German, published two volumes on the parables (*Die Gleichnisreden Jesu*, 1888-9). He helped to move the interpretation of parables in the right direction by insisting that each parable story has one basic lesson that needs to be discovered. Jülicher tended to find moral lessons and may not always have identified the basic teaching of parables correctly. He may have been too restrictive; some parables seem to have more than one prong. Yet his was a more healthy approach than treating parables as allegory.

In the English-speaking world, Professor C. H. Dodd published his *Parables of the Kingdom* (1937). He stressed that all the parables of Jesus relate to Jesus' basic message, the kingdom of God. The parables illustrate the many aspects of this kingdom that Jesus has brought. Dodd has been criticized because he overemphasized the presence of the kingdom and did not leave enough room for the future dimension of the kingdom of God.

Another German, Joachim Jeremias, also made a contribution to interpreting the parables by publishing his *Die Gleichnisse Jesu* (1947). He stressed the importance of putting the parables into their original Palestinian setting. Since then, many volumes on the parables have been published, building on the work of these pioneers. Scholars have learned that it is not always easy to identify the central thrust of all the parables of Jesus. When that point is identified correctly, these seemingly innocent tales often have a very sharp point.

Why Did Jesus Use Parables? They were a popular teaching method in his day. Jewish rabbis were known to teach with parables. Parables make abstract truths concrete. In a parable, the hearer is confronted with a truth and must respond. Jesus did not use parables to make his message abstruse or complicated but to make it plainer.

That statement raises the question about the meaning of Mark 4:10-12, where Jesus says, "For those outside, everything comes in parables; in order that 'they may indeed look, but not perceive, and may indeed listen, but not understand; so that they may not turn again and be forgiven.' "

Some critics insist that these cannot be words of Jesus and that they must have been put in his mouth by the early church. But that approach takes us in a wrong direction.

Instead, we must ask whether Jesus actually meant to blind people by speaking in parables. In that same chapter of Mark, we read, "With many such parables he spoke the word to them, as they were able to hear it; he did not speak to them except in parables, but he explained everything in private to his disciples" (4:33-34). From these verses, we must conclude that parables were designed to make the teachings of Jesus about the kingdom of God easier to grasp. Jesus was willing to explain the parables further to those who followed him into a house.

It is not quite clear how Mark uses the Greek word *hina* ("in order that," 4:12, NRSV), as he begins to quote or adapt Isaiah 6:9-10. Are we to understand it as introducing a purpose clause? In that case, Jesus says, "In order that they . . . may not turn again and be forgiven"!

Some scholars read it in a causal sense: "Because they look but do not perceive, and listen but do not understand," they are not converted. In the parallel to this passage in Matthew 13:13, we have *hoti*, instead of *hina,* and that may mean "because." Still others have understood *hina* in a relativistic sense. "For those outside everything comes in parables." They look but do not perceive, listen but do not understand, and so are not converted.

Perhaps it is best if we understand *hina* (in order that) as shorthand for introducing fulfillment of the OT: "In order that it might be fulfilled what Isaiah said." In other words, what happened in the days of Isaiah the prophet, is happening again in the case of Jesus. People are hearing God's message, but they refuse to receive it, and that leads to the hardening of the heart.

When we recall that *parabolē* has a wider meaning, then we can read the entire text something like this: "To you [the disciples] has been given [by God] the secret of the kingdom of God [he has revealed it to them]. But for those on the outside [the unbelievers], everything comes in "riddles" [they are puzzled]. And so what Isaiah said is being fulfilled once again: they may indeed look, but not perceive, and may indeed listen, but not understand; so that they may not turn again and be forgiven."

By using the parabolic method, Jesus tries to make

the message of the kingdom of God as clear as he can. But as in the days of Isaiah, people again close their hearts to the message, and then it makes no sense. When people listen with open hearts, their minds are able to grasp what Jesus is saying to them. Then they can confess their sins and be converted.

Subthemes in the Parables. The fundamental message of the parables is that of the inbreaking and presence of the kingdom of God. In the parables many aspects of this main theme are touched upon.

• Some of Jesus' parables are messages of divine grace. Examples are the parables of the lost sheep, the lost coin, and the lost son (Luke 15); the parable of the Pharisee and the tax collector (Luke 18); the parable of the two debtors (Luke 7); the parable of the workers in the vineyard (Matt. 20); and others.

• Several parables speak of the growth of the kingdom of God. We have the parable of the seed growing secretly (Mark 4); the parables of the leaven and of the mustard seed (Matt. 13).

• Some parables speak of the discovery of the kingdom of God, such as the parable of the treasure in the field, and the parable of the precious pearl (Matt. 13).

• Certain parables teach us how disciples of Jesus, who belong to the kingdom of God, should live. There is Jesus' parable of the friend at midnight (Luke 11), on persistence in prayer; or the parable of the unforgiving servant (Matt. 18), which underscores the importance of forgiveness. We have parables on stewardship, such as the parable of the unjust steward (Luke 16), and that of the rich man and Lazarus (Luke 16). The parable of the good Samaritan teaches Christ's followers how to respond to the needy (Luke 10).

• As mentioned earlier, there are also parables that portray the future of the kingdom of God, particularly the judgment at the end of this age. We see this in the parable of the ten maidens (Matt. 25), the sheep and the goats (Matt. 25), the wheat and the weeds (Matt. 13), the dragnet (Matt. 13), and others.

There are other ways of classifying the parables. Nevertheless, all of them are related to the central message of Jesus, the kingdom of God.

What is important in our attempts at understanding the parables is that we try to familiarize ourselves with the customs and practices of Jesus' day. If, for example, we know something about the farming methods in Palestine in the first century, we will better understand the parable of the sower and the seed (Mark 4). Some knowledge of the pastoral life of Israel will help us understand the parable of the sheep and the goats.

Familiarity with Jewish marriage customs of that day goes a long way in interpreting the parable of the ten maidens. Many of the parables of Jesus have their setting in the fishing industry, the household, the economy, or other aspects of Palestinian life. Hence, it is important that we become acquainted with the Jewish culture of Jesus' day.

The parables were spoken by Jesus to a particular audience. When our Gospels were written a generation or so later, our four Evangelists had different audiences in mind. So we must ask, first of all, What did Jesus want to convey to his audiences in his day? Then we must inquire, What did Matthew, Mark, and Luke want to convey to their readers? Finally, we face the question: What is this or that parable saying to us today?

Acts

Literary parallels to our Gospels are tough to identify, but history writing was a well-known practice. It would probably be an oversimplification if we called Acts a history book. It is also full of theology. So perhaps we should see it as theological history.

In the history of the NT canon, Acts played an important role. The Gospels close with the resurrection of our Lord; Luke alone mentions his ascension (24:51), and it appears in the longer ending of Mark (16:19). Readers of the Gospel accounts naturally ask, What happened after the resurrection? Acts gives the answer to that question.

Those who read the letters of the NT also want to know the origins of the churches to which the apostles are writing. Again, Acts gives us information.

In the formation of the NT canon, Acts, appropriately, has become the connecting link between the Gospels and the epistles.

Acts describes the founding and the early days of the church. Hence, churches have tried from time to time to go back to the early church and to find there the exact model for restoring the church today. We can surely learn much from the early church. But the church that came into being at Pentecost continued to grow and develop. At the end of the apostolic era, it was no longer exactly as it was when it began.

Moreover, there are certain unique and unrepeatable first-century events that later churches cannot imitate. Narrative literature often has lessons to teach us that are implicit and not clearly spelled out. So we must be somewhat cautious in claiming that Acts teaches us this or that.

In the Sinaiticus manuscript of the NT, Acts is called simply *Praxeis* (Acts). Literature by that name was well-known in the first century. For example, there were the "Acts" (*Praxeis*) of Alexander the Great. The book of Acts, however, presents much more than an account of the acts of the apostles, for the book also contains many speeches. Furthermore, in the book, the church expands through the initiative of the Holy Spirit, so some say it should be called the Acts of the Holy Spirit.

The title "Acts" is not part of the original text. As time passed, the simple title "Acts" was lengthened to read "Acts of Apostles," and even "Acts of All the Apostles." Yet Luke does not report the acts of all the apostles. Basically we have the acts of two apostles, Peter and Paul. Chapters 1-12 are overshadowed by the acts and speeches of Peter. The rest of the book features the acts and speeches of Paul.

It looks as if Luke wanted to show parallels between these two leading apostles. Peter heals a cripple (Acts 3:2-8), and so does Paul (14:8-10). Peter confronts a former magician (8:18), and we have a similar event with Paul (13:6). Peter raises Tabitha from death (9:40); Paul raises Eutychus (20:9-10). Peter is freed from prison in a miraculous way (12:7-11), and so is Paul (16:25-31). In light of such parallels, we may be tempted to call the book the Acts of Peter and Paul, but the Greek manuscripts do not use this title.

When we seek to interpret the book of Acts and ask how to apply this book to the life of the church today, we face a number of problems. Acts describes a pioneer situation. That means we can never duplicate exactly what the early church did. In those days, when the gospel was proclaimed and people were converted, the leaders immediately baptized them.

Churches today may allow for a waiting period in which new converts are instructed in the Christian faith. That would not violate the spirit of the NT, even though such a practice is nowhere explicitly mentioned.

The picture also changes in the case of children who grow up in Christian homes. At an early age, they may accept the Christian faith but are not yet mature enough to take the step of baptism and function as members of the church. Hence, the church may postpone baptism until they are ready to take this important step.

Theologically, however, conversion, receiving the Holy Spirit, and baptism all go together.

Nothing is said in Acts about constructing church buildings, since the early church met in homes. We look in vain, then, for explicit instruction on building places of worship. We shouldn't try to justify erecting costly churches from the OT story of building the temple. Nothing is said in Acts about music or choirs or worship teams. But again, the church is not bound to limit its practices to only those mentioned in the book of Acts.

Hence, not everything mentioned in Acts is normative for us today. We see this in chapter 8, where the conversion of the Samaritans is reported. In his Pentecost speech, Peter had promised that those who repent and believe will receive the gift of the Holy Spirit. This did not happen immediately when the Samaritans believed and were baptized.

Philip had preached the gospel. The Samaritans accepted it and were baptized with water. The Spirit, however, was delayed until Peter and John came down and witnessed the coming of the Spirit upon the Samaritans. It was important for the apostles to witness this event, lest they should have any doubts about the genuineness of the faith of these despised people.

For the Samaritans, the presence of the apostles must have been quite meaningful. After that they could think of themselves as members of the apostolic church. Reading this account should not lead us wrongly to conclude that there are two stages to Christian conversion. It does not mean that baptized believers today lack something and must have another postconversion experience.

The experience of the Samaritans was unique and

must not be held up as normative for converts to Christianity in our day. If that were attempted, we would have great difficulty with other passages in Acts in which people's conversion experiences are described in rather different ways.

Note also that the early church was under the leadership of the apostles. We know relatively little about the activity of most of the apostles in the post-Pentecost period. But the apostles clearly were the foundation and the early leaders of the church being built by Jesus (Eph. 2:20; Matt. 16:18) through the work of the Spirit (Acts 2).

Some time later, the church in Jerusalem was led by elders, among whom James seems to have been the leader. Elders can be replaced and have to be replaced when they die, but apostles cannot be replaced. They are the foundation of the church, and we have no apostles today in the primary sense of that word. For that reason, church leaders today dare not presume to have the same authority that the apostles exercised.

From time to time, churches meet in conventions today to deal with issues that arise in the life of the church. Yet they cannot take the Jerusalem Council meeting, described in Acts 15, as their model in every respect. We do not have apostles today as they did in the first century.

It is also important to observe developments in the early church. The churches that were planted all over the Roman empire did not all imitate precisely what the Jerusalem mother church did.

Even today, Hutterites insist on practicing community of goods, and that is their privilege. But it cannot be proved that this was the practice in all first-century churches. What we can learn from the early church is to be willing to sacrifice earthly possessions for the sake of the needy. Yet such giving must be voluntary, as it was then.

It is commendable that Barnabas sold a field and took the proceeds to the apostles (Acts 4:36-37). In the next chapter, Peter affirms the right of Ananias and Sapphira to their own property (5:4). Mary, the mother of Mark, owned a house large enough for the early church to use as a meeting place (12:12). Paul exhorts those with material possessions to be generous (Rom. 12:8; 2 Cor. 8), but nowhere does he encourage a wholesale liquidation of all property.

Pentecost, like the cross and the resurrection, is foundational to the Christian faith. These saving events are unique and cannot be repeated in Christian experience. Therefore, we cannot, like the 120 in the upper room, imitate them and continue in prayer until the Spirit is poured out on our lives, as it was on the day of Pentecost.

Even the speaking in tongues at Pentecost was unique. It enabled people from various places in the empire to hear the word of God in their native dialects. Quite different is the gift of tongues as mentioned by Paul in 1 Corinthians 12–14. There tongues enabled believers to commune with God, but in a way not understood by others. An interpreter was needed (14:27-28), the opposite of Acts 2, where people understood.

Many questions the early church faced are not our questions today. Some of the early church's questions had to do with its emergence in a Jewish milieu.

What should be the church's position with respect to the synagogue, the temple, the Sabbath, and other Jewish practices? How should the Hellenists and Hebraists live together in fellowship in the church? What are Christians to make of the OT dietary laws? Should circumcision be required of male believers from the Gentiles?

As the gospel spread to lands outside of Palestine, other questions had to be faced. What, for example, should be the attitude of believers toward meat that had been routinely dedicated to idols? These and many other issues are not the church's questions in our North American setting today. We can still learn important lessons from the way these issues were handled in the early church. Yet we cannot always apply the accounts in Acts directly to the church today.

Over the centuries, churches have developed different forms of worship, different teaching and preaching methods (such as Sunday schools, Bible schools, seminaries, etc.), and different organizational structures. Such changes and innovations may be made in the spirit of the NT.

We must, however, be careful not to say that our way of doing things is "the" biblical way, for all churches tend to be selective in their reading of the book of Acts. On the other hand, no true church can ever afford to cut itself off from its historical roots, found in this key document of the NT.

Letters

Of the twenty-seven books of the NT, twenty-one are in letter or epistle form. If we add the seven letters embedded in the last book of the Bible, we have a total of twenty-eight letters. Although it is hard to identify a gospel genre before the coming of Christ, there certainly was a wealth of epistolary literature available. Discoveries of secular letters in the sands of Egypt, written on papyrus, have demonstrated that the letter form, as we have it in the NT, was well-known.

In the sacred literature of other great religions, the letter form is not used. Likewise, no book of the OT is in letter form. But the NT has many epistles. They are usually divided into two categories: the letters of Paul, and the general epistles or catholic (meaning *universal*) epistles. They are called this because they have no specific address.

General Observations. In form, the letters of the NT are similar to secular letters. Here is an example: "Irenaeus to Apollinarius, his dearest brother: Many greetings. I pray continually for your health." The writer begins with his name, and then gives us the name of the recipient. Next comes the greeting, and then the prayer. That's not too different in form from the letters of Paul, though he uses Christian vocabulary. Moreover, he writes as an apostle inspired by the Spirit of God.

As for the number of Pauline letters, there is some question. Hebrews is anonymous, but we know that Paul wrote more than the thirteen letters that mention him as author. There is the so-called lost letter, mentioned in 1 Corinthians 5:9. In Colossians 4:16 (CEV) Paul mentions the letter he wrote to Laodicea, which we do not have. He probably wrote some other letters, but we do not have them.

In his letters, Paul addresses the needs of congregations, many of which he had founded. But there are also the more private letters to Timothy, Titus, and Philemon. Paul wasn't always sure that the churches would read his letters, as we can see from his exhortation in 1 Thessalonians 5:27. His letters are occasional letters: there was some occasion that gave rise to them.

What seems strange is that Luke, who honors Paul's mission to the nations, never mentions any of Paul's letters in his long account about Paul. Luke does present a letter giving the decree from the Jerusalem Council. Paul and company take it to Antioch and read it to the church (Acts 15:23-31; cf. 21:25). After Paul is in custody at Jerusalem, the tribune sends a letter with him to Felix in Caesarea (23:25-35). So Luke knows it is a common practice to send letters.

It is possible that the publication of Acts stimulated the collection of the Pauline letters. In our canon today, his letters are arranged in decreasing order of length, with the church letters first, followed by the private letters.

Besides the thirteen Pauline letters we have eight other apostolic epistles in the NT, written by Peter, John, James, and Jude, and the unknown author of the epistle to the Hebrews. These general epistles do not have the traditional letter form, and some of them must be viewed as tracts, treatises, or sermons.

As for the composition of the Pauline letters, it looks as if the apostle dictated them. In the case of his letter to the Romans, he even mentions the amanuensis or scribe (Rom. 16:22). In several letters he makes reference to his signature (1 Cor. 16:21; Col. 4:18; 2 Thess. 3:17). Paul even calls attention to the large letters with which he wrote the conclusion to Galatians (6:11), distinguished from the smaller letters of a trained scribe. Whether the secretaries to whom Paul dictated his letters affected the style of his writing is not altogether certain.

Paul writes in the Koiné (common) Greek spoken in the lands surrounding the Mediterranean. However, since he was a Hebrew, his Greek style is influenced by his Semitic background, somewhat like the Greek OT. His Greek vocabulary often carries Semitic connotations.

Paul uses figurative language quite liberally. His imagery is drawn from the city, the farm, the military, the building trade, the sports world, Jewish religious practices, the sea, and so forth.

Since letters of private individuals were not delivered by the imperial post, Paul had to find friends who were willing to serve as letter carriers. In several of his epistles, he names those who delivered his letters—

Titus (2 Cor. 7:7-8), Epaphroditus (Phil. 2:25), Tychicus (Col. 4:7-9; Eph. 6:21-22). Obviously, it often took considerable time for his letters to be delivered.

Hermeneutical Considerations. Someone has compared the letters of the NT to a telephone call where we eavesdrop on only one side of the conversation. We second-guess what is being said at the other end of the line. In similar fashion, we can partly guess what questions or problems Paul addresses by the answers he gives.

Many issues to which Paul spoke in his letters are different from the ones we face today. Hence, we cannot carry over everything he says directly to our situation. However, even though much of what Paul wrote is limited by time and place, there are basic biblical teachings in his writings that are applicable in all generations.

When, for example, Paul advises Timothy to drink a bit of wine for the sake of his stomach (1 Tim. 5:23), that had a personal, direct, but a time-bound significance. Yet even in such personal exhortations, we can find abiding principles. Such an advice need not be taken to encourage the drinking of alcoholic beverages. But it does legitimize the use of medicine to improve health.

Paul asks Timothy to bring with him the cloak he left in Troas, as well as the books and especially the parchments (2 Tim. 4:13). We all know that such a request cannot be carried over directly to any or all situations in the life of the church or of individuals.

Yet even in a request like this, we can see Paul's humanity: he is concerned about the coming winter and wants his coat. He also admits that he needs the help of others. Paul is concerned about his spiritual and mental life; he wants his books. (This verse kept John Darby from selling his library!)

In North America, we are not commonly faced with the question of eating meat offered to idols (1 Cor. 8–10;

Rom. 14). But we still have to deal with questions of conscience. These chapters give believers important guidelines in that area of their Christian life. The problem Paul addresses raises the whole question of Christian freedom. We need to relate helpfully to others who have different views regarding some ethical matters. Paul encourages us to "pursue what makes for peace and for mutual upbuilding" (Rom. 14:19).

Paul's controversy with those Jewish Christians who insisted on the practice of circumcision is not one that concerns us today. But we are still faced with a similar question: What do we require of converts if they want to become members of our own congregations (assuming that we practice believers baptism)?

Paul rejects circumcision as a requirement for salvation. He thus reminds us that our salvation does not rest on works but on the grace of God alone.

In several of his letters, Paul addresses problems related to slavery. Our society has outlawed slavery, though sometimes cases still crop up in North America, and we may notice instances of economic slavery. Have these Pauline passages nothing to say to us? We cannot carry them over directly to the relationship of employer to employee. But in a general sense, Paul tells both Christian masters and slaves things that apply to Christian employers and employees.

The churches Paul founded had to contend with developing gnosticism, cults holding that matter is evil and salvation comes through esoteric knowledge. That may not be our problem today. But we can learn from the apostle how to view ideologies that degrade the human body, treat the human spirit as divine, or skew the NT teachings to discount the human nature of our Lord. From Paul's combat against gnostic tendencies, we can see that believers are always in danger of mixing up current opinions with the teachings of the Scripture.

When churches today find themselves in situations similar to ones addressed in the NT letters, it is easier to carry over teachings of the apostles more directly. First Peter, for example, can easily be understood by churches undergoing persecution in our day. This holds true also for many of the words of comfort, assurance, and warning contained throughout the epistolary literature. Many of the ethical instructions (vices prohibited, virtues commended) can also be carried over directly to the life of the church today. When Paul condemns the "works of the flesh," we know that these sins are wrong always and everywhere.

We should not, however, expect the first-century apostles directly to address some of the ethical problems the church faces in the twentieth century. Yet there are guiding principles to be found in the NT letters. These principles can be applied to many of the ethical issues with which the church has to contend from time to time.

The apostle John exhorts believers not to love the world, meaning everything alienated from God (1 John 2:15). This is a command that needs to be applied in new ways in every generation. Paul calls on his Galatian readers to manifest the fruit of the Spirit (Gal. 5:22). We may have a problem with practicing these graces, but surely they pose no problem of interpretation.

Apocalyptic

The Literary Genre. In the last book of the Bible, we find a type of literature known as apocalyptic. The first word of the book is the Greek word *apokalupsis* (revelation, unveiling). A powerful vision of the risen Lord (Rev. 1) sets the scene for the Lord's letters to the seven churches (Rev. 2–3).

God's "servant John" (1:1) calls his message to the

churches "words of the prophecy" or "the prophecy of this book" (22:7-21). Prophets speak to the needs of people—comforting, warning, exhorting, and threatening. They have a profound pastoral concern for the people they are addressing.

Much of the book of Revelation, however, is apocalyptic in style. In literature of this type, the focus is on God's reign, the ultimate outcome of history, and the call to be faithful through persecution. There is a sense of urgency in preparation for the end of the age, marked in Revelation by the return of Christ (1:3; 22:7, 12, 20).

Apocalyptic was a type of literature well-known in Judaism. Daniel is the only apocalyptic book in the OT, though there are other passages showing a development from prophecy to apocalyptic (such as Isa. 26:7-19; visions in Ezek. and Zech.). A considerable amount of apocalyptic material has been preserved in the Apocrypha (2 Esdras or 4 Ezra) and Pseudepigrapha (as in 1-2 Enoch, 2-3 Baruch, Jubilees, Apoc. of Abraham). The apostle John, then, did not need to create this literary genre. Instead, he made use of this literary style to convey Christian messages.

Jewish apocalyptic is generally quite pessimistic. Hope for world betterment has been abandoned, and the present is dark. There's little point in trying to improve our current situation. The end is around the corner, when God will impose judgment and end the age. Even the hope of a restored nation of Israel is often lacking in Jewish apocalyptic (but note God's renewed kingship in Dan. 2:44; 7:27; Zech. 14:9).

Apocalyptic writers tell about dreams and visions they have had or about messages given to them by angels. In conveying their messages, they make generous use of symbolism. Sometimes they even draw upon mythological imagery to express some truth about

God's dealings with the world.

In Jewish apocalyptic, God's plan for this evil world is typically seen as fixed. History is moving steadfastly to an end, and there is little that humans can do about it.

In prophecy, on the other hand, there is always an element of hope: if people repent and return to the covenant, then God promises to restore them and bless them (2 Chron. 7:14; Ezek. 18:21). However, that note of hope is mostly lacking in Jewish apocalyptic, which tends to regard history as fixed and determined by God. Instead, it tends to be somewhat deterministic. There is a great interest in calculating the time of "the decreed end" (Dan. 9:27; cf. 7:25; 8:14; 12:6-12).

Outside the OT, Jewish apocalyptic is pseudonymous. The writers assume the name of some worthy person in Israel's sacred history. They write in the names of Adam, Abraham, Enoch, Moses, and others. This gave their messages greater authority and, by hiding their identity, they shielded themselves against attacks.

The book of Revelation has many similarities with Jewish apocalyptic literature. However, it is thoroughly Christian in its orientation. In addition, John does not need to use a pen name: he is a prisoner of Rome on the isle of Patmos.

Jewish apocalypses were said to be "sealed" (Dan. 12:9), since they were open only to an elite class of readers who had the wisdom to understand them. But John's Apocalypse is to be read in the churches and is to be understood by ordinary members of the church (Rev. 1–3). His book concludes with the exhortation "Do not seal up the words of the prophecy of this book" (22:10).

In contrast to the typical pessimism of Jewish apocalyptic books, Revelation is basically quite optimistic. The glorious end of human history has been determined at the cross, where Christ won the victory over all evil powers. Although the church must suffer for a season, victory is assured; it is only a matter of a short time, and Christ will return in great glory and take his own home to Mount Zion.

John opens up to us the deep caverns of human wickedness. He is a realist, but he never loses sight of the triumph of the Lamb that was slain.

Revelation is basically a book of comfort. John writes to suffering Christians and assures them that in God's own time they will be glorified.

The government of this world is not in the hands of fate, but in the hands of the One who sits upon the throne (Rev. 4:10). The church may have to suffer sometimes throughout this period of waiting, but it is under divine protection, and God limits the time of suffering (12:6, 12). Believers have God's mark on them (14:1), and God knows who belongs to him. He will bring his own through the dark valleys of this earth to the new Jerusalem (21–22).

Hermeneutical Questions. Revelation has been interpreted in many ways in the long history of the church. These interpretations seem to follow along the following lines:

The Contemporary-Historical Interpretation. Many interpret the book in the context of the first century. That is, of course, where we must begin if we want to understand any book of the NT. In the case of the Apocalypse, however, we cannot limit the message of the book to the first century. John also looks into the future and depicts the church's lot between Pentecost and parousia.

The Historicist Interpretation. This method seeks to find the fulfillment of what the apostle wrote in the events of history, beginning in the first century. For example, the immoral woman, sitting on the Beast (chap. 17) is taken by some to be the medieval church with its seat in Rome. The swallowing of the open booklet (chap. 10) is supposed to be a reference to the Protestant Reformation, when the Scriptures were "opened" once again.

Some see the emergence of demonic locusts from the abyss as a reference to the French Revolution (9:3-11). When ten European countries joined the European Union, some Bible readers saw in that the fulfillment of the reference to the ten kings aligned with the beast (17:12). And so it goes. Such interpretations are, however, completely artificial and arbitrary.

If the book is not seen as a panorama of human history from the first century onward, then at least the seven letters to the churches are seen as addressing different periods of the church. The letter to Ephesus, then, reflects the first-century church, and the letter to Laodicea is a picture of the church in the days just prior to the return of Christ. The other five letters are allotted to other periods of the church's history.

In reply, there is nothing in the history of the church that allows this kind of distribution of the letters. They were all written to first-century churches as were all the other letters of the NT. We must now seek to understand their messages and apply them to churches everywhere in every generation. Moreover, it would be exceedingly sad and rather hopeless if the entire church in the days prior to Christ's coming should be depicted as Laodicean in character.

The Futuristic Interpretation. According to this method of interpretation, John is describing the dark days the church will have to endure in the days just prior to Christ's return. Although the letters to the seven churches have a first-century context, the rest of the book is projected to the end of human history, a time of great tribulation. When this time of trouble is over, Christ will return in great glory and inaugurate his millennial reign on earth, after which the people of God enter their eternal home.

This line of interpretation has some legitimacy but tends to misrepresent the meaning of expression "the last days." According to NT writers, the last days began with Pentecost and continue throughout this time of waiting. They must not be understood as a reference to the brief period just prior to Christ's return. If that is so, the book has relevance for the life of the church throughout history, from Pentecost to parousia.

The Dispensational Interpretation. According to the teachings of John Darby, the Lord returns twice at the end of the age. First he comes for the rapture of the church. Then, after a period of tribulation, he returns with his church to reign on earth for a thousand years.

In this method of interpretation, only the first three chapters of Revelation are directly applicable to the church today. With the beginning of chapter 4, the church is said to be with the Lord. The scenes of judgment described throughout the book are supposed to depict the great tribulation. People left on this earth must endure that suffering under antichrist's reign, after the church has been raptured.

There are differences of opinion on the length of that tribulation. A popular view, taking a number out of the book of Daniel, is seven years. At the end of this dark period, antichrist is judged and the millennium follows.

This line of thinking, however, is plagued by serious problems. First, the NT does not teach two returns of Christ. Moreover, there is nothing in the NT to suggest that the church will be spared tribulation. The church has suffered from time to time throughout human history and will continue to do so until the end.

This view also robs the church of the great lessons taught in Revelation 4–19. According to dispensational thinking, those chapters describe the great tribulation following the rapture of the church. But it is not right to excise whole blocks of NT material and say that they do not apply to the church today.

The Symbolist Interpretation. In a sense all the previous views also take seriously the symbolism of the Revelation. Yet in this method of interpreting the book, we are not concerned about what the book meant in the first century or, for that matter, in any other century. Instead, interpreters seek to identify the permanent religious truths of the book, represented by the varied imagery of apocalyptic language. This approach, however, is not firmly anchored in history.

All of the above ways of interpreting Revelation have something to be said in their favor. However, one method alone can never do justice to this great book. The Apocalypse will yield its treasures only when various methods are combined.

As in the case of other NT books, we must always first ask, What did the writer want to tell the churches of the first century? Then we ask, What is the message of this book for us today? In that way the interpretation is anchored in first-century history, but it also remains relevant for the church in all ages.

By taking the different literary genres of the NT books into account, we have gone a long distance toward interpreting them correctly.

12

The OT in the NT

*T*he OT was the Bible of Jesus and the apostles. They quote these Scriptures and apply them in an amazing variety of ways. The coming of Jesus, his life and teachings, and above all, his death and resurrection, gave the NT writers a new standpoint from which to read the OT.

In Jewish synagogues, the apostle Paul made many converts by reinterpreting the OT in the light of Christ. When proclaiming the good news to Gentiles, as in Paul's sermon on the Areopagus, Christian missionaries did not quote the OT quite so freely (Acts 17:22-31; cf. 14:15-18).

OT quotations in the Greek NT may appear in the form of a free translation of the Hebrew text. Often the apostolic writers quote the Greek version of the OT (the Septuagint). Even that version may be adapted upon occasion to suit the new situation. Here and there, they may be quoting Aramaic Targums. These are Aramaic paraphrases of the Hebrew text, first oral in the synagogue and later written (cf. Neh. 8:7-8, with the oral Aramaic interpretation of the Hebrew being read).

It is estimated that about one-tenth of the NT is comprised of OT material. Some editions of the Greek NT print OT quotations in bold print, to give the reader a feeling for the great amount of OT material in the NT. OT quotations are particularly numerous in Romans, Hebrews, and Revelation.

NT Quoting OT

According to one count, there are 295 explicit quotations from the OT in the NT. Some of them occur more than once, but about 278 are singular. Of these 278 quotations, 94 come from the Torah, 99 from the Prophets, and 85 from the Writings (the three divisions of the Hebrew Bible; cf. Luke 24:44). Of the 39 books of the OT (as in English Bibles), 9 are never quoted (Judg., Ruth, Song of Sol., Eccles., Esther, Ezra, Neh., 1–2 Chron.). Job is quoted only once (1 Cor. 3:19).

From the way NT writers introduce OT texts, one can see how highly the Jewish Scriptures were valued by Jesus and the apostles. Some of the formulas with which they introduce a quotation were also used by Jewish writers (such as "it is written," "the Scripture says," "the law says," etc.).

Frequently the apostles personify OT Scripture:

• "As the scripture has said, . . ." (John 7:38).

• "The scripture, foreseeing that God would justify the Gentiles by faith, declared the gospel beforehand to Abraham, saying . . ." (Gal. 3:8).

These are just two examples of personification—the Scripture speaks, it foresees, it declares.

Sometimes the speaking of the Scriptures and the speaking of God are identified: "For the scripture says to Pharaoh, 'I [God] have raised you up for the very purpose of showing my power in you'" (Rom. 9:17). When the Scripture speaks, God speaks.

Some quotations explicitly state this:

• "Have you not read that the one who made them at the beginning made them male and female, and said, 'For this reason a man shall leave his father and mother and be joined to his wife'?" (Matt. 19:5).

• "Sovereign Lord, . . . it is you who said by the Holy Spirit through our ancestor David, your servant: 'Why did the Gentiles rage . . . ?'" (Acts 4:24-25).

• "For to which of the angels did God ever say, 'You are my Son; today I have begotten you?'" (Heb. 1:5).

• "As the Holy Spirit says, 'Today, if you hear his voice . . .'" (Heb. 3:7).

In these and other passages, God and the Scriptures are identified.

In some cases, the NT names the OT author through whom God spoke: Moses, David, Isaiah, Jeremiah, Daniel, Joel, and Hosea. Not only are human authors mentioned, but occasionally the Holy Spirit is named as the source of the saying (as in Mark 12:36; Acts 1:16; 4:25; 28:25; Heb. 3:7; 9:8; 10:15).

In this chapter, we want to see how Jesus and the apostles made use of the OT. First, we give illustrations of OT quotations in the NT. Then we shall see how Jesus and the NT writers apply the OT to the new situation brought about by the coming of Jesus. As interpreters of the Bible, it is our task to discover how Jesus and the apostles used the OT.

More often than not, Jesus and the apostles quote single verses (the OT was not yet versified as our Bibles are). Sometimes they quote several OT passages in a cluster. In Romans 10, for example, we have three quotations in succession, taken from the Writings (Rom. 10:18; Ps. 19:4), the Law (Rom. 10:19; Deut. 32:21), and the Prophets (Rom. 10:20-21; Isa. 65:1-2).

We may have a combination of texts from different parts of one OT book (e.g., John 12:38-40; Isa. 53:1; 6:10). Another cluster of OT texts is found in 2 Corinthians 6:16-18 (6:16 from Lev. 26:12; Jer. 32:38; Ezek. 37:27. Then 2 Cor. 6:17 from Isa. 52:11; Ezek. 20:34, 41. Finally, 2 Cor. 6:18 from 2 Sam. 7:14; Isa. 43:6; Jer. 31:9).

Behind such clustering of passages stands the emphasis in the OT that all testimony is to be supported by two or three witnesses. Sometimes passages found in different books of the OT are combined and quoted as coming from one author. We shall illustrate how the NT writers quote the OT in the examples below.

Mark 1:2-3. "As it is written in the prophet Isaiah, 'See, I am sending my messenger ahead of you, who will prepare your way; the voice of one crying out in the wilderness: 'Prepare the way of the Lord, make his paths straight.' "

Mark wants to anchor his message in the Holy Scriptures. So he opens his Gospel with quotations from the OT. The first quotation (1:2) is in part from Malachi 3:1 and from Exodus 23:20; only in verse 3 do we find a quotation from Isaiah 40:3. Yet the entire quotation is cited as coming from Isaiah.

Later copyists found this to be a problem, so we have manuscripts omitting "Isaiah" and citing "prophets." They were protecting Mark from being accused of error. But such a correction was unnecessary. It was already a practice in Judaism to combine passages and give the name of only one author. Mark doesn't have to mention all of his sources; he mentions only Isaiah, even though he draws upon other books.

Moreover, he adapts these quotations to fit the new situation. In Malachi we read that the messenger will prepare "the way before me" (God), but Mark changes that to "you," to apply it to Christ. Since he speaks of preparing the way, he naturally thinks of the exodus from Egypt (Exod. 23:20) and of Isaiah 40:3. In both of their original contexts, God is preparing the way for his people, after delivering them from bondage. John the Baptist will do the same for people in spiritual bondage.

In the quotation from Isaiah, Mark also makes adjustments. Isaiah 40:3 reads, "In the wilderness prepare the way of the Lord [God], make straight in the desert a highway for our God." Mark changes the last part of that verse to "make *his* [Messiah's] paths straight."

What may have led Mark to combine these three passages is the fact that in all of them the wilderness plays a role. Israel leaves Egypt to journey through the wilderness. Israel leaves Babylon to go home to Judea through the wilderness. And John the Baptist is in the wilderness preparing the way for the Messiah. In all of them, we have the theme of deliverance from bondage, as well as that of a messenger who proclaims freedom to God's captive people.

Matthew 1:22-23. "All this took place to fulfill what had been spoken by the Lord through the prophet: 'Look, the virgin shall conceive and bear a son, and they shall name him Emmanuel,' which means, 'God is with us.' " (Greek: Emmanuel = Hebrew: Immanuel.)

Matthew sees the birth of Jesus as the fulfillment of OT prophecy. In his Gospel, Matthew uses the formula "so that it might be fulfilled" fourteen times. Sometimes he quotes OT texts without this formula. In 1:22-23, Matthew repeats words that Isaiah spoke to King Ahaz in the eighth century B.C. (Isa. 7:14).

At that time, Jerusalem was threatened by enemies from the north, Israel and Syria. Through Isaiah, the Lord told the king to request a sign that God would deliver Judah from her enemies. But Ahaz refused to ask for a sign. In response, the prophet told Ahaz that God would give him a sign anyhow: a young woman would bear a son, and he would be called "Immanuel." Before that child is old enough to make moral decisions (age 12 or so?), Judah's enemies, Israel and Syria, will be overrun by Assyria. Judah will survive, but with hardship.

First, we note that Matthew quotes the Greek OT,

which has the word *parthenos*, usually meaning "virgin" (but not in Gen. 34:3). The Hebrew text has *'almah*, which means "a young woman" who may or may not be a virgin. In Hebrew, the word for "virgin" is *bethulah*. As evident in 1:18-25, Matthew clearly holds to the virgin conception of Jesus (and so did Luke).

In Isaiah 7:14, it is not so evident that the eighth-century young woman is a virgin. Perhaps the text means a young woman untouched by a man before the act of conceiving.

We also do not know which woman Isaiah has in mind (cf. Isa. 8:3-8). But Isaiah assures Ahaz that the birth of a son will be a sign that God is with Judah. So the child should be called "Immanuel," meaning "God is with us."

That promise, first given to Ahaz in a dark moment of Judah's history, is now applied in a new way. Joseph, too, has entered a dark hour; he has just discovered that Mary, his betrothed, is pregnant. Just then a heavenly messenger appears and gives him the same promise that Isaiah gave Ahaz eight centuries earlier. The new application of that promise is called a fulfillment: "The virgin shall conceive and bear a son, and they shall name him 'Emmanuel.'"

Again, as in the Marcan text above, Matthew gives this quotation from Isaiah 7:14 in slightly different form. In Isaiah we read, "The young woman . . . shall name him Immanuel." Matthew 1:23 says, "*They* shall name him Emmanuel." "They" refers to the new people of God whom this son, who is about to be born, will save from their sins (Matt. 1:21).

Acts 15:15-18. "This agrees with the words of the prophets, as it is written, 'After this I will return, and I will rebuild the dwelling of David, which has fallen; from its ruins I will rebuild it, and I will set it up, so that all other peoples may seek the Lord—even all the Gentiles over whom my name has been called. Thus says the Lord, who has been making these things known from long ago.'"

Representatives of the Antioch church had come to Jerusalem to discuss whether Gentile men who became Christians should be required to be circumcised. At this meeting Peter makes his position clear: Gentiles should not be asked to take on circumcision. Paul and Barnabas speak in favor of Peter's position. All of them have witnessed the conversion of Gentiles.

Finally, James gives his opinion on the matter. As far as we know, he has not personally engaged in a mission to Gentiles, but he argues against requiring circumcision on biblical grounds. James quotes Amos 9:11-12 as in the Greek OT, where the prophet foretells the restoration of the ruined dwelling of David. The Hebrew text of Amos 9:11-12 is quite different: "In order that they may possess the remnant of Edom and all the nations who are called by my name, says the Lord who does this."

We do not know in which language James speaks when he addresses the assembly, but the quotation from Amos is like the Septuagint (Greek OT). If he spoke in Aramaic, then Luke has given us the passage in Greek. The Hebrew text clearly speaks of the restoration of national Israel. James, however, interprets the rebuilding of the house of David in a spiritual sense; for him, it means the conversion of the Gentiles.

Why the Septuagint translators changed "Edom" to "Adam" (man) is not known. Edom and Adam were occasionally confused. Before the introduction of vowel points into the Hebrew text, only the consonants were written, and Edom and Adam have the same consonants. More problematic is the change of the verb (*yarash*) "possess" (Amos 9:12) to (*darash*) "seek" (Acts 15:17). Instead of "possessing" the remnants of Edom, we now have "seek the Lord."

In whatever way we might explain the differences between the Hebrew and the Greek texts of the Amos passage, one thing is clear: James understood Amos to anticipate the day when Gentiles would become members of the people of God. For him, their conversion, without the requirement of circumcision, was the way God was rebuilding the ruined house of David.

Therefore, according to James, it has been perfectly legitimate for Peter, Paul, and Barnabas to take the gospel to the Gentiles, for they are fulfilling OT prophecy. Right at the end of his argument, as reported by Luke in Acts 15:17-18, James quotes a saying from Isaiah 45:21, "known from long ago." In other words, God had foreseen the salvation of the Gentiles long ago.

Ephesians 4:8. "Therefore it is said, 'When he ascended on high he made captivity itself a captive; he gave gifts to his people.'"

This is a quotation from Psalm 68:18, which in the Hebrew Bible reads: "You ascended the high mount, leading captives in your train and receiving gifts from people, even from those who rebel against the Lord God's abiding there."

Paul quotes this word from the psalm to describe Christ's triumph over all evil powers. Having completed his work of redemption here on earth, he has ascended victoriously to heaven. As Conqueror, he now distributes the booty of the war, as it were, to his followers; he gives them gifts.

The quotation is introduced with the Greek formula *legei*, which can mean "it says" or "he says" or "she says." If "it" (or "she") is correct, then Scripture (*graphē* is feminine in Greek) is here personified as speaking, though it could also refer to the Holy Spirit (*pneuma* is neuter in Greek). If "he" is the better translation, then the verse refers to God or the psalmist David speaking.

But what is said? In this case the apostle is not quoting the Septuagint and is not strictly translating the Hebrew text of the psalm into Greek. The Hebrew text tells of the royal conqueror leading captives in his train and "receiving" gifts of (or from) men (people). Paul says that he "gave" gifts to men (people). The Septuagint is quite similar to the Hebrew.

Scholars have long noticed that the way Paul quotes the passage from Psalm 68 is like the Targum (Aramaic paraphrases given orally in the synagogue and later written). The Targum of Psalm 68:18 is closer to what Paul says than either the Hebrew or the Greek OT texts.

In fact, there was a rabbinic interpretation of the psalm holding that Moses was the one who had ascended on high and then gave the law as a gift to God's people. At the time of the apostles, the Pentecost festival in Judaism was a celebration of the giving of the Law at Sinai.

Paul may have these Jewish traditions in mind when he writes Ephesians and describes the triumph of Christ. He speaks of the glorious exaltation of our Lord, who poured out his Spirit at Pentecost and thereby enriched the new people of God with spiritual gifts.

It is possible, however, that Paul is simply thinking of the triumphant return of Israel's king from battle. After the king comes home with much booty, he lets his followers have a share. In any case, Paul does not need to quote the psalm verbatim. Neither is he bound to quote it the way translators turned the Hebrew text into Greek (in the Septuagint). He may simply have taken the imagery of Psalm 69:18 and adjusted it to fit the new situation.

At times the writers of the NT seem simply to borrow their language from the OT texts, without giving them in the form in which they are found in the Hebrew Bible.

The above examples from the Gospels, Acts, and Epistles illustrate the way apostolic writers quote the OT. However, the use of the OT in the NT goes far beyond quotations. Hence, we need to consider the application of the OT to the new situation, brought about by the coming of the Savior of the world.

Jesus challenges his contemporaries, many of whom are avid students of the Scriptures, to discover him in their own sacred writings: "You search the scriptures because you think that in them you have eternal life; and it is they that testify on my behalf. Yet you refuse to come to me to have life" (John 5:39-40).

NT Applying OT to New Situations

By Jesus, as Reported by the Evangelist

Jesus saw a resemblance between himself and certain OT individuals, events, experiences, and historical situations.

OT Personages and Events Prefigured Christ. Jonah, for example, was miraculously delivered from death and through his preaching led the Ninevites to repentance. Jesus will in due time be authenticated through an even greater deliverance, by his resurrection from the dead. But because his contemporaries refuse to receive his message, their condemnation will be greater.

The antitype (fulfillment) is always greater than the type: "Something greater than Jonah is here!" (Matt. 12:39-41). This is immediately followed by a reference to the queen of Sheba, who came from the ends of the earth to listen to the wisdom of Solomon. But many of Jesus' contemporaries refuse his message, even though "something greater than Solomon is here!" (Matt. 12:42).

Jesus defends his disciples when they have plucked heads of grain on a Sabbath because they were hungry. He refers to David, who also did something not normally allowed. David and his companions ate the bread of the Presence, which was to be consumed only by the priests (Mark 2:25-26; 1 Sam. 21:1-6).

The priests also performed certain temple duties on the Sabbath. Yet they were not considered to be Sabbath breakers. "I tell you, something greater than the temple is here" (Matt. 12:5-6).

When Jesus began his public ministry in his hometown of Nazareth, he compared himself with the OT prophets Elijah and Elisha. These prophets, who were not accepted by their contemporaries, were sent to the widow in Sidon and to Naaman the Syrian, both outsiders. In similar fashion, Jesus was rejected by the people of Nazareth (Luke 4:24-27).

On another occasion, Jesus identified himself with Isaiah the prophet. When his message was rejected, Isaiah felt as if he had been called to harden people's hearts instead of leading them to repentance (Mark 4:12; Isa. 6:9-10).

Experiences of OT Israel Applied to Christ. When the devil tempts Jesus in the wilderness, our Lord responds to every temptation with a saying from the OT (Deut. 8:3; Ps. 91:11-12; Deut. 6:16). All these quotations have their setting in the wilderness journey, when Israel was tested and taught (Matt. 4; Luke 4).

Jesus predicts his death and the resurrection that is to follow in three days. In doing so, he not only recalls the experience of Jonah in the belly of the fish, but possibly also Hosea 6:2: "On the third day he will raise us up." Although the prophet had a national renewal in mind, it appears to be a close verbal parallel to Jesus' prediction of his own resurrection (Mark 8:31; cf. John 2:19-21).

In the passion narrative are repeated references to the innocent sufferings of the OT psalmists, with which our Lord identifies. In John 13:18, when he predicts his betrayal by Judas, he is reminded of Psalm 41:9: "Even my bosom friend in whom I trusted, who ate of my bread, has lifted the heel against me." While Christ suffers agony in Gethsemane, he thinks of the psalmist who asked himself, "Why are you cast down, O my soul?" (Ps. 42.5, 11; 43:5; Mark 14:34). When he hangs on the cross and utters his cry of dereliction, it is in the words of the suffering psalmist: "My God, my God, why have you forsaken me?" (Ps. 22:1; Mark 15:34).

OT Prototypes of Jesus' Contemporaries. Jesus sees a parallel between his contemporaries and the hypocrisy and shallowness of Israel in the days of Isaiah. "Isaiah prophesied rightly of you hypocrites, as it is written, 'This people honors me with their lips, but their hearts are far from me' " (Mark 7:6; Isa. 29:13, Greek OT). What the prophet said of apostate Israel in his day, Jesus applies to his own countrymen.

Moses called the Israel of his day "a perverse and faithless generation." Jesus uses that language to describe his own generation (Deut. 32:5; Matt. 17:17). In fact, he foresees the judgment of God coming upon his unbelieving contemporaries and describes it in categories used by the prophets, as illustrated below.

The day will come, says Hosea, when Israel will call on the mountains to cover them. That is what Jesus says will happen in the coming catastrophe that leads to the destruction of Jerusalem (Hos. 10:8; Luke 23:30).

"Your house shall be left desolate," says Jesus (Matt. 23:38). This is similar to Jeremiah 22:5, where the prophet announces judgment on the temple. Jerusalem would be trampled upon, said the prophets (Isa. 63:18;

Dan. 8:13). That's also what Jesus says of the holy city (Luke 21:24).

These examples (and many more) illustrate Jesus' practice of taking OT persons, events, attitudes, and experiences, and applying them to the new situation brought about by his coming. They embody a principle being repeated in Jesus' ministry.

Jesus stands in line with the OT, and he gives it a christological interpretation. Of course, it is not simply a repeat performance, for Jesus is the greater one. Jesus Christ is the fulfillment of the OT. He ushers in the messianic age. That marks the beginning of a new people of God in whom the hopes of the OT are being fulfilled.

OT Predictions. There are many passages in the OT that take on new meaning in the light of Christ's coming. Sometimes they are in the form of a prediction; at other times they are simply typological, supplying a type that is fulfilled in Christ and the church. It is not always easy to distinguish between these two. Sometimes Jesus simply uses OT language to describe the new situation. The predictive passages are found primarily in Isaiah, Zechariah, the Psalms, and Daniel.

The OT predicts the coming reign of the son of David. This reign will be ushered in by some savior figure. The predominant conception of *messiah* is that of an ideal king (Ps. 110:1; Mark 12:36). The Messiah is not only the Son of David (Mark 10:47), but also David's Lord (Matt. 22:42-45).

Jesus is the stone falling, crushing, and/or tripping his enemies (Isa. 8:14-15; Dan. 2:34ff.; Luke 20:18). He is the "Branch" who will rebuild the temple (Zech. 6:12-13; Mark 14:58). Jesus is the King who rides humbly on a donkey (Zech. 9:9; Mark 11:1ff.). He is the Shepherd whom wicked people strike, scattering the sheep (Zech. 13:7; Mark 14:27).

The predictions of messianic salvation are also fulfilled in Jesus. He establishes a new covenant, anticipated by Jeremiah (Jer. 31:31; Luke 22:20). Jesus is the true Shepherd who seeks the lost (Ezek. 34:16, 22; Luke 15:1-7; 19:10). He is the suffering servant, who dies for the many (Isa. 53; Mark 10:45). He is the Son of Man coming in clouds of glory to receive dominion (Dan. 7:13-14; Mark 14:62).

Jesus combines what the OT predicted about the son of David, meaning the ideal king, and the suffering servant who dies for his people to atone for their sins. Generally, the theologians of Jesus' day think of Messiah in terms of Davidic kingship (viewed rather nationalistically). They overlook the suffering and death of God's servant. But these two lines of prophecy are brought together already at Jesus' baptism.

When Jesus is baptized by John, the voice from heaven announces, "You are my Son, the Beloved; with you I am well pleased" (Mark 1:11). This is a combination of Psalm 2:7, where Davidic sonship is mentioned, and Isaiah 42:1, speaking of the suffering servant with whom God is pleased.

From these examples, we see that the teachings of Jesus are permeated with OT types, predictions, images, or simply with OT phraseology. This no doubt has encouraged the Evangelists and apostles to do the same. Let us look at a few illustrations from the Gospels and the epistles.

By Evangelists and Apostles

It would take us too far afield if we were to survey all of our Gospels. Hence, we limit ourselves to Matthew for illustrative purposes.

Matthew. We have already described how Matthew sees the fulfillment of Isaiah 7:14 in the birth of Jesus (Matt. 1:23). In Matthew 2:15, the Evangelist sees the fulfillment of Hosea 11:1, "Out of Egypt have I called my son" (referring to Exod. 4:22).

The weeping mothers of Judah, whose children were massacred by Herod's decree, remind the Evangelist of Judah taken captive to Babylon. He imagines Rachel in her grave, weeping for her children (Jer. 31:15; Matt. 2:18).

The birth of Jesus in Bethlehem recalls Micah's prophecy (Mic. 5:2; Matt. 2:6). Matthew makes a significant change in the Micah text by underscoring that Bethlehem is "by no means" the least among the rulers of Judah.

Later, Jesus departs from Nazareth and begins his ministry in Capernaum. This reminds Matthew of Isaiah 9:1-2, saying that the land of Zebulun and Naphtali by the sea, where people sat in darkness, now see a great light (Matt. 4:15-16).

What is said of the suffering servant in Isaiah 53:4, that he has borne our infirmities and carried our diseases, is applied to the healing ministry of Jesus (Matt. 8:17). The manner in which the suffering servant carries out his mission (Isa. 42:1-3), is reflected in Jesus' ministry (Matt. 12:18-19).

When our Lord teaches in parables, Matthew is reminded of Psalm 78:2, "I will open my mouth in parables" (Matt. 13:34-35).

Jesus' entry into Jerusalem (Matt. 21:5-9) is described in terms taken from Zechariah 9:9. The thirty pieces of silver, thrown down in the temple (Matt. 27:3-10), are like the wage given to the shepherd (Zech. 11:12-13). God commanded Jeremiah to buy a field, even when the Babylonians were knocking on the gates of Jerusalem (Jer. 32:6-12). The blood money returned by Judas is applied to purchasing the potter's field (Matt. 27:10).

Besides these quotations, the Gospels are full of allusions to the OT. For example, the Fourth Evangelist says of Christ, "The word became flesh and tented among us" (John 1:14, author's trans.). He is alluding to God dwelling in the tabernacle in the midst of his people Israel.

The Baptist points to Jesus and declares, "Behold, the Lamb of God" (John 1:29, KJV). He is thereby alluding to the paschal lamb of the exodus (Exod. 12).

Jesus, when conversing with the Samaritan woman at the well, offers her living water (John 4:1-42). This is reminiscent of the many appearances of God or an angel (theophanies) in the OT that occur at wells.

Thus it goes, both in John and in the Synoptics. To catch these allusions, one has to be familiar with the OT.

Paul. The apostle has a high view of the OT. It represents the very oracles of God (Rom. 3:1-2). All Scripture is, in his view, inspired by God (*theopneustos*) (2 Tim. 3:16). The most common formula used for introducing OT texts is "it stands written" (*gegraptai*) (29 times) or "the scripture says" (6 times). Beyond that there is great variety in Paul.

In his method of quoting the OT, the apostle is not different from his Jewish contemporaries. However, in his interpretation, he parts company with them. In the light of the Christ event and the illumination of the Holy Spirit, the OT takes on a new meaning for Paul.

In Ephesians, Paul says, "You have already heard . . . how the mystery was made known to me by revelation, as I wrote above in a few words, a reading of which will enable you to perceive my understanding of the mystery of Christ. In former generations this mystery was not made known to humankind, as it has now been revealed to his holy apostles and prophets by the Spirit" (Eph. 3:2-5).

Every significant conception in Paul's theology has

its roots in the OT. Sometimes it's hard to say whether he is consciously quoting or unconsciously alluding to the OT. One might go so far as to say that the entire NT is a reinterpretation of the Old. After all, the apostles see in the Christian church the fulfillment of the OT hopes.

Paul gives the OT a christological interpretation. His theology is steeped in OT thought, and so are his ethical teachings. A few illustrations of these two areas from the writings of Paul might be helpful.

Paul's Theology. The apostle's doctrine of God is that of the OT: "There is no God but one" (1 Cor. 8:4). This is an allusion to the Shema, Israel's confession of faith (Deut. 6:4).

Not only the unity of God, but also his fatherhood has OT roots, though it is given a new interpretation. In the OT, God is Father in the sense of the Creator—not only of the whole world, but also of the people of Israel. In the NT, God is not only the Father of our Lord Jesus Christ, but also the Father of all believers, who call him *Abba* (Aramaic: Father; Rom. 8:14-15; Gal. 4:6).

In Paul's theology, God is also the Creator of all things (Rom. 1:25; Eph. 3:9; 1 Tim. 4:3). What is new is that God created this universe through the agency of Jesus Christ (Col. 1:16; 1 Cor. 8:6; cf. John 1:3; Heb. 1:2).

Paul's doctrine of justification by faith is a theme well-known since the days of the patriarch Abraham. He expounds this doctrine particularly in the epistles of Romans and Galatians.

Abraham is the father and prototype of all believers. He is that spiritual tree into which Gentile believers, the wild branches, have been grafted (Rom. 11:17-24). A true Jew is no longer one who is a Jew outwardly, but one who is a Jew inwardly—a true child of Abraham (Rom. 2:28-29; cf. Gal. 6:15-16; 3:7).

Paul's view of the law, so central in Jewish thought,

is also modified in the light of Christ. Faith, he argues, came before the law. The law given 430 years later cannot annul the covenant God made with Abraham, based on faith (Gal. 3:15-18).

The law is holy, to be sure, and it is an important guide to holy living, but it was never designed to be the basis for justification before God. Works are important, but they spring from faith, as in the case of Abraham. Works are not the means by which we can earn our salvation (Eph. 2:8-10).

Even the doctrine of the church has its roots in the OT. In the Greek OT, the people of God are frequently designated as the *ekklēsia* (assembly), which becomes the standard word for the new people of God. They are the church, the descendants of Abraham (Gal. 3:29) and the Israel of God (6:16). Believers are the true circumcision (Phil. 3:3), the peculiar people (Tit. 2:14, KJV).

The church has gained a share in the heritage of ancient Israel—not ethnic Israel, but spiritual Israel. Isaac and Ishmael were both physical descendants of Abraham. But only Isaac had the faith of Abraham. Jacob and Esau were both descendants of Isaac, but only Jacob was his spiritual descendant. Even when the nation of Israel became apostate, there was always a true people of God, a faithful remnant (Isa. 37:31-32; Jer. 23:3). The church stands in continuity with that genuine people of God.

Paul's calling to bring the gospel to the nations also had its validation in the OT Scriptures. He defends his Gentile mission with passages such as Romans 9:25: "Those who were not my people I will call 'my people,' and her who was not beloved I will called 'beloved.'" That passage is similar to Hosea 2:23.

In Romans 10:20, Paul uses another passage from the prophets (Isa. 65:1) to legitimize his Gentile mission: "I have been found by those who did not seek me; I have shown myself to those who did not ask for me." In Romans 15:9-12, Paul quotes four passages from different parts of the OT in support of his mission to the Gentiles.

In Romans 10:21, Paul mourns the rejection of the gospel by his own people in words similar to Isaiah 65:2: "All day long I have held out my hands to a disobedient and contrary people."

His teaching on final judgment also has its roots in the OT concept of the day of the Lord. Paul takes a new step in identifying this day of the Lord with the *parousia* (second coming) of Jesus Christ (2 Thess. 2:1-2). The day of the Lord, as the prophet Amos already indicated, will be a dark day, a day of judgment, for the ungodly. But it will be a day of deliverance for the true people of God (1 Thess. 1:10; 5:3, 9-10).

Thus, Paul's theology is firmly rooted in the OT. His ethical teachings are also informed by the Jewish Scriptures.

Paul's Ethical Teachings. Paul teaches that we should love our enemies. He finds support for a nonvindictive spirit in Leviticus 19:18: Paul quotes from Deuteronomy 32:35 in Romans 12:19-20: "Vengeance is mine, I will repay."

Paul exhorts believers to love their neighbors, for all God's commands are summed up in this word, "Love your neighbor as yourself" (Rom. 13:9; Lev. 19:18).

Paul uses language from Genesis 2:24 in his warnings against sexual sins. He reminds them, "The two shall be one flesh" (1 Cor. 6:16). His encouragement to support God's servants financially (1 Cor. 9:9) finds support in the OT law that forbids muzzling the ox (Deut. 25:4).

Paul even builds on the sad history of Israel's failures

during the wilderness journey (1 Cor. 10:1-15). It serves him as he strongly warns the Corinthians not to fall into the same trap: "These things occurred as examples for us, so that we might not desire evil as they did" (1 Cor. 10:6).

In arguing for Christian liberty in the matter of meat offered to idols, Paul refers to Psalm 24:1, the Jewish table prayer: "The earth and its fullness are the Lord's" (1 Cor. 10:26).

Differences between male and female are attributed to the Creator's design (1 Cor. 11:1-16; Gen. 1:26-28: 2:15-24).

The separation of believers from the evil world system has its precedents in the OT; God dwells among his people (2 Cor. 6:16; Exod. 25:8; Lev. 26:12).

Christian generosity in giving is supported by OT texts: "The one who had much did not have too much, and the one who had little did not have too little" (2 Cor. 8:15; Exod. 16:18). "He scatters abroad, he gives to the poor; his righteousness endures forever" (2 Cor. 9:9; Ps. 112:9).

One can hardly think of an area of Christian ethics that is not informed by the OT.

The OT was Paul's Bible. His experience on the Damascus Road, where he met the risen Christ, radically altered his understanding of the Bible, but it did not lessen its importance for him. His knowledge of Christ gives him a perspective from which he can penetrate the true meaning of the OT. What we have said about Paul can be said of all the other apostles as well.

The apostles indicate that the OT writers did not always fully grasp what their oracles meant, as 1 Peter 1:10-11 suggests. The *sensus plenior*, the fuller meaning, could be understood only from the standpoint of later developments. That does not mean, however, that the new applications of the OT texts, as found in the writings of Evangelists and apostles, rob these passages of their original meaning.

The NT writers are so immersed in the language of the OT that sometimes they simply use the language of the Jewish Scriptures to express themselves.

Bible readers still puzzle over the significance of the OT for the life and ministry of the church. To help us understand the relationship of the OT to the New, we must think in terms of God's progressive revelation in the history of salvation.

13

Progressive Revelation and the Unity of the Bible

*T*here are significant differences between the books of the OT and those of NT. The OT books were written in Semitic languages, the NT books in Hellenistic Greek. The OT spans a thousand-year history of the people of Israel, beginning with the exodus from Egypt, up through the return from Babylonian exile. In addition, it presents the patriarchal period, in Genesis 11 to 50.

The OT books focus on the history of a people chosen by God to be his covenant people and called to carry out God's saving purposes in human history. The NT books, by contrast, grew out of the new covenant, established by Christ through his death and resurrection, with a new people of God. In this new people, all racial and national boundaries are transcended.

In spite of these profound differences, there are strands of teaching in both Testaments that provide for continuity in God's plan of redemption. In biblical interpretation, we must constantly wrestle with elements of continuity and the elements of discontinuity between the two Testaments. When these are not observed, we can easily confuse the voice of God in the Scriptures with that of our own human understanding.

Does the patriarchal practice of polygamy legitimize

such a practice today? Is it proper to derive the notion of the divine right of kings, found in the OT, as a legitimate form of government? Can we today condone the OT sanction of killing witches? Does the OT prohibition of usury forbid us to collect interest on our savings today? Does the prediction that women will suffer pain in childbirth forbid Christian women the use of pain-killing drugs in childbirth today? Because tithing was the law in Israel, does that mean it is a law for Christians?

These and similar questions call for sound hermeneutics when we face the question of continuity versus discontinuity between the two Testaments. When progressive revelation was not taken seriously, almost anything could be justified by the Bible. Shakespeare describes this practice in *The Merchant of Venice:* "In religion, what damned error, but some sober brow will bless it and approve it with a text, hiding the grossness with fair ornament" (act 3, scene 2).

Progressive revelation is a view that is validated by the writers of the NT. The unknown author of the epistle to the Hebrews writes, "Long ago God spoke to our ancestors in many and various ways by the prophets, but in these last days he has spoken to us by a Son" (1:1-2a). The same God who spoke to the patriarchs and who spoke through the mouths of the prophets has in the last days spoken to us by his Son, Jesus Christ.

There is thus a unity in the divine revelation to which the books of both the Old and the NT witness. But there is also a progression in God's revelation that reached its climax in Christ, who is both the Alpha and Omega of all of God's purposes. Hence, as we interpret the books of the Bible that give us the earlier revelation of God, we must do so in light of the fuller and final revelation given to us in the books of the NT.

The NT Witness to Progressive Revelation

Some scholars object to the expression "progressive revelation." They prefer to speak of God adapting his messages to both the earlier and later historical situations in which the readers of the Scriptures found themselves. Some scholars prefer to speak of "cumulative revelation."

Sometimes the word *progressive* is misconstrued to suggest an evolution of religious thinking in Israel. Primitive ideas eventually give way to more advanced thought. But we are not using the word *progressive* in the sense of an evolution of religious ideas in Israel. Instead, we are using it to claim that God, in his infinite wisdom, made himself known from earliest times. Then in the fullness of time, he sent his Son, who revealed to us God's saving plans in a fuller way (Gal. 4:4-5).

By progressive revelation, we mean that God made himself known in stages, and the final stage was reached in Christ. The earlier stages of divine revelation must be understood in the clearer light of that final revelation.

Repeatedly the NT writers speak of the fulfillment of the Scriptures. "When the fullness of time had come, God sent his Son, born of a woman, born under the law" (Gal. 4:4). In Ephesians 1:10, Paul says that in Christ, God has gathered all things in heaven and earth. The different fractions of salvation history have, in other words, found a common denominator in Christ, and now they make better sense. In Christ, says Paul, all the promises of God are Yes and Amen (2 Cor. 1:20).

To the Corinthians, Paul writes that the ends (*telē*) of the ages have come upon them (1 Cor. 10:11). The church stands at the climax of God's inscrutable salvatory ways, and even heavenly beings are learning something of "the wisdom of God in its rich variety" as they observe the new people of God (Eph. 3:10).

The sermons of the apostles, as recorded by Luke in the book of Acts, also reflect progressive revelation. They begin somewhere in Israel's early history and walk the hearers through several stages of God's redeeming acts. Then they always conclude with the finished work of Christ and the offer of salvation.

Along the same line, Rick Johnson comments:

> The limitation of the OT as Christian Scripture, however, derives from the new revelation of God in Jesus Christ. Because this new revelation has been given, the older one can only be judged incomplete. It is authoritative but its authority must be interpreted in the light of the new word. This is why Jesus can go beyond Moses on questions such as divorce, swearing, or retaliation (Matt. 5:31-42)." (Corley: 114)

That leads us to consider how progressive revelation affects our hermeneutics.

Exegesis and Progressive Revelation

Since the OT belongs to the period of preparation, we cannot take a passage from any book and say, "This is what the Bible teaches." Some biblical teachings are found only in bud in the OT; the full flowering appears in the NT. For example, the OT says almost nothing about life in the world to come.

It is important also to recognize that the people of God in the OT are a national entity, a nation state. Many of the laws of the OT pertain to life in such a setting. There is a whole body of civil law that hardly applies to the church, even though there may be much there that modern states might imitate for the good of the people.

But certainly no modern farmer feels bound to let his land lie fallow every seventh year.

Many wrong applications of OT texts have been made because OT and NT were seen as lying on a plane. However, the view that everything taught in the OT is applicable to the new people of God, the church, gets us into trouble. Some scholars have suggested that only OT teachings endorsed in the NT are applicable. Others hold that everything in the OT is applicable to the church if it is not reversed in the NT. A better approach is to view the OT in the light of the final revelation in Christ.

This has implications for the concept of a state church, a concept as old as the fourth century. Sadly, this concept was perpetuated by the mainline Reformers in the sixteenth century and supported from the OT.

Whether to have a state church or a voluntary free church was one of the major issues on which the Anabaptists parted company with the medieval church and with the mainline Reformers. Anabaptists held that in Christ a new people of God had emerged that was completely transnational.

Pilgram Marpeck (1490-1556) taught that just as the foundation must be distinguished from the house, so the OT must be distinguished from the NT. He argued that we should not give the preliminary word of God (the OT) the same authority as the final Word (Jesus Christ).

Anabaptists made much of the fact that there were *two* covenants—the old and the new. We might think they were extreme in their view of progressive revelation, but they were reacting against the misuses of the OT. It is not hard to find illustrations showing how OT texts were abused.

When European settlers established themselves in

North America, they often thought of themselves as the new Israel, taking over the land of Canaan. That meant they could treat the natives as Israel was commanded to treat the sinful Canaanites.

Priests in the OT were to wear special clothing, so the ministers of some churches had to have distinctive clothes. Solomon's temple was often taken to be the prototype of the cathedral or an excuse for building costly houses of worship. The principle of circumcision in the OT was supposedly perpetuated by infant baptism. David danced before the Lord, and that was sometimes used as a model for Christian worship.

Some people have tried to apply the OT law of retribution to the church in a rigid fashion. God promised Israel that if they would remain true to the covenant, he would bless them materially. If they were unfaithful, they would suffer the consequences. However, this teaching led to real problems already in OT times when this law was applied to the individual, as we can see in Job, in Psalm 73, and in other OT texts.

NT believers have also applied this law frequently to their own lives and found that often it didn't seem to work. Godly people do experience tragedy and loss, become ill, and sometimes die young.

This problem becomes acute when people apply verses such as 2 Chronicles 7:14 to a nation or to an individual: "If my people who are called by my name humble themselves, pray, seek my face, and turn from their wicked ways, then I will hear from heaven, and will forgive their sin and heal their land."

In a general sense, it is true that a nation respecting the laws of God will be better off than one in which wickedness and injustice are allowed to flourish. But we must not rigidly apply the OT law of retribution to the individual. Jesus taught us better. When the disciples saw a man born blind, they asked him, "Who sinned, this man or his parents?" Jesus responded by explaining that neither of them had sinned. Instead, this was an opportunity for the works of God to be revealed in the blind man (John 9:1-3).

Not only do we see progressive revelation when OT and NT are compared; within a Testament we may also detect some progressive revelation and growing insight.

For example, Jesus told Nicodemus that he had to be born of *water* (baptism) and Spirit if he wanted to enter the kingdom of God (John 3:5).

We have to ask, "What might *water* have meant for Nicodemus?" Since he was a rabbi and knew Ezekiel 36:24ff., he likely understood water in terms of that text: "I will sprinkle clean water upon you, and you shall be clean from all your uncleannesses. . . . A new heart I will give you, and new spirit I will put within you."

Christian readers would take John 3:5 as a reference to baptism (cf. 1:33). In Ephesians 5:26, however, Paul mentions "the washing of *water* by the word," to be purified and set apart for Christ.

On the Christian view of the state, we should not read only Romans 13, where obedience to government is ordered. We must also read Revelation 13, where the state has become beastly and believers are persecuted by the state and suffer innocently for the faith.

Particularly in questions of ethics, we need to wrestle with progressive revelation.

Pre-Christian Ethics and Progressive Revelation

Some OT saints engage in practices clearly condemned in the NT (if not already condemned in the OT). Abraham, the spiritual father of all believers, is less than truthful in his relations with Pharaoh and with

Abimelech. To protect his visitors, "righteous" Lot offers his virgin daughters to the men of Sodom. We might also think of the many evils that plagued the house of Jacob. The Judah and Tamar affair would be a case in point.

When we come to the book of Judges, it seems as if Israel has hit bottom in the matter of moral behavior. Even the story of Esther raises ethical questions, when she prepares her body for twelve months in anticipation of her first night with the king.

We have questions about some of the family practices in the OT (such as polygamy). The law permitting divorce also is problematic, as we can see from Jesus' comments (Deut. 24; Mark 10:4ff.). Then there is God's command to exterminate the Canaanites and even capital punishment for a rebellious son.

How do we handle such matters in the light of the NT? Can we still hold to the unity of the Bible when there seem to be such apparent differences between the two Testaments? In the past, Christians repeatedly found some of the ethical practices mentioned in the OT to be convenient, giving legitimacy to some of their own questionable practices.

Jan van Leyden, who tried to establish a Christian kingdom in Münster, advised men to have more than one wife because so many men had been killed in battle. He used the precedent for this in the lives of the patriarchs. Martin Luther permitted Philip of Hesse to have two wives on the same OT grounds. Luther condemned divorce, but in this case allowed bigamy.

In a sense, it is refreshing to see how realistic the biblical writers are when they report questionable acts in the lives of OT believers. It strengthens our confidence in the trustworthiness of the Bible since it does not conceal the failures. It also reminds us that salvation did not come through a spiritually elite class of people but by God's grace. God used fallible human beings as agents to bring the light of salvation to our world.

Christians who read the OT sometimes try to overlook the ethical failures of OT believers or even to excuse them. A Christian publication printed a sermon on "Abraham, the Model for God's Servants." In it the preacher suggested that Abraham's deception, when he lied to Pharaoh, implied that God's servants also should be "creative." But when the writers of the OT books told rather embarrassing stories about some of the heroes of faith, they intended to warn us. They did not want us to imitate those failures.

Certainly no sane person would come to the conclusion that the sad affair of David and Bathsheba was recorded so that we might have an example to follow. David's repentance after his fall into sin makes that clear. Some events serve as warnings, to instruct us (1 Cor. 10:1-13).

In some cases, when OT believers sinned, they almost immediately received divine judgment. We might mention Gehazi, who lied and was punished with leprosy (2 Kings 5:19-27).

There are ethical violations that can be attributed in part to oriental customs. Solomon's harem probably was more of a demonstration of his political greatness than his immorality. He overlooked the fact that these foreign wives brought their idolatrous practices with them. This obviously says something about Solomon's lack of spiritual perception.

Pacifists have found Israel's wars to be problematic. But war and bloodshed are not really God's will. David, for example, was denied the privilege of building the temple because he had too much blood on his hands. Jehu's house was punished because of the brutal manner in which he had treated Ahab's family.

However, in the matter of the conquest of the land of Canaan, we do have a direct command from God. This war was unique; it was "holy war" (Lind). The fall of Jericho is a good example. It is worth noting, however, that after Israel became a nation "like other nations" and had a professional army, God never again commanded Israel to go to war. The conquest of Canaan has to be understood as God's provision of a land for his people, and as God's judgment upon the idolatrous Canaanites (Exod. 3:8; 23:23-33; 34:11-16; Deut. 32:34-43; Josh. 3:10).

Jesus and the apostles also taught that the wicked were subject to divine judgment and wrath (Matt. 11:22; Rom. 1:18). Yet they emphatically taught and lived out love for enemies. The NT writers do not call on believers to enact God's judgment, and they are not to use force and bloodshed. They are to feed their enemies and leave vengeance in God's hands (Rom. 12:17-21; on this passage, see chap. 6, above).

In any case, the ethics of the OT must be viewed in the light of the NT. That, however, does not mean that there is a lack of unity in God's plan of salvation. This unity has been understood in a variety of ways in Christian history. Some attempts to explain the unity of the Bible have been more successful than others. Let me mention a few of them!

Attempts to Relate OT and NT

Allegory. Allegory (see chap. 8) was rather popular in the early centuries of the Christian era, particularly in Alexandria. It was a method of interpretation already at home in Judaism, and Christians borrowed this method.

In Antioch, there was greater emphasis on the literal interpretation of Scripture and considerable resistance to allegorizing interpretation. Christian interpreters who made use of the allegorical method often simply read NT truths into OT texts and thereby "Christianized" them.

We occasionally find this practice even among twentieth-century believers. Some spin out fantastic interpretations of the OT tabernacle and its furnishings—even the arrangement of the furniture suggests the cross to some readers. Whenever wood is mentioned or the color red occurs, some devout reader will interpret the text to be a reference to the cross.

The Song of Solomon is a poem on human love. Yet it has frequently been interpreted allegorically as depicting the intimate relationship between Christ and his bride, the church. How arbitrary this approach is can be seen when the breasts of the beloved are interpreted to mean OT and NT, from which the believer draws nourishment. Allegory does not help us understand the unity of the Bible; it artificially imposes NT truths onto OT texts.

Typology. Here we are on firmer ground, for the NT endorses the typological interpretation of the OT.

Typology is not prophecy. Instead, a person, event, or action that has no explicit connection to the future is later understood to have pointed forward to the new age that dawned with the coming of Christ. Typology is a theological interpretation of the OT on the part of the apostolic writers. In the OT, the early church and the NT writers saw types of the birth, the ministry, the death, and the exaltation of Jesus; the mission of the church; and the day of the Lord at the end of the age.

Not every character, thing, or event in the OT is to be understood typologically. But when viewed from the standpoint of progressive revelation, we can see many types in the OT. There is a big difference between allegory and typology: in typology the literal meaning of the OT texts is taken seriously. But in the light of the fuller revelation that followed, readers can see how persons and events pointed to what was to come.

OT characters (such as Melchizedek) are types of Christ. Prophets (Deut. 18:15), priests (Heb. 4:14), and kings (Ps. 2:6) point to the coming Messiah. Events, such as the exodus, are types of the salvation that is ours in Christ.

Thus, the lifting up of the brazen serpent is a type of Christ being lifted up (Num. 21:8-9; John 3:14). Abraham's life as a sojourner is a type of the people of God who are not at home in this world (Heb. 11:13:16). Jonah's experience in the belly of the great fish is a type of Christ's burial and his resurrection after three days (Matt. 12:40).

If there were no fundamental unity between the two Testaments, it would hardly be fair to engage in typological interpretation. There is, however, no unanimity among Bible scholars on the limits of typology. Some wish to restrict themselves to types mentioned explicitly as such in the NT. Others go to the other extreme and sometimes cross over into allegory.

For example, Noah's ark becomes a type of the church (cf. 1 Pet. 3:20-21). From that people infer that, just as the ark was preserved in the Flood, so the church will be kept from the tribulation. Cyprian, a church father, even suggested that only those who were members in the established church of his day (in the ark) would be saved in the end. Outside the church was no salvation.

In the Middle Ages, it occurred to some astute theologians that since Noah took both clean and unclean animals into the ark, so the church should have room for both saints and sinners. They claimed that Jesus supported this view in a parable about weeds growing among the wheat in the field: "Let them both grow together until the harvest" (Matt. 13:30). Church discipline, in that case, would be unnecessary. But in 13:38, Jesus says, "The field is the world."

Thematic Unity. Many take another way of approaching the question of the unity of the Scriptures. They isolate basic themes found in both Testaments. For example, in both Testaments we have the same God. The God of Abraham, Isaac, and Jacob, is the God of our Lord Jesus Christ. This God revealed himself long ago to the people of Israel, and in a fuller sense revealed himself in Jesus Christ.

It is also clear from both Testaments that God loves the world and is at work, carrying out plans of redemption for all humanity. Even though he seems to restrict his revelation to Israel in earlier times, it is clear from the OT that he wants to save the whole world. Israel is chosen to be his instrument to carry out this universal plan of salvation.

It is another matter to recognize that Israel has failed to share the knowledge of God's salvation with the rest of the world. But even when the nation of Israel became apostate, there was always a faithful remnant, a people of God who remained true to the covenant. Through this "holy remnant," God carried his purposes forward (Isa. 6:13; 11:11-12). God's saving plans, not always explicit in the OT, were fully revealed when he sent his Son to be the "Savior of the world" (John 4:42).

When we say that the same God is at work in both OT and NT to bring about salvation for humanity, we immediately touch another major theme that ties the two Testaments together: the people of God. In the OT, this people is still ethnically defined. But right from the beginning of salvation history, it becomes clear that it is not to remain limited by race. Israel was chosen to become the receiving station of the waves of eternity and then, in turn, Israel was to broadcast them all over the world (Gen. 12:3; Exod. 19:6; Isa. 42:6; 49:6).

The OT gives clues that some people from other nations joined the covenant with the Lord (as in Exod. 12:38; 20:10; Josh. 6:22-25; Ruth; 1 Sam. 26:6; 2 Sam. 11:3). Yet on the whole, Israel failed in carrying out its mission to the nations.

The book of Jonah is the sharpest criticism of such failure. Jonah speaks powerfully of God's love for all the people of this world, including wicked Nineveh. Even when the leaders and most of the people in the Northern Kingdom became apostate, there were seven thousand who had not bowed their knees to Baal (1 Kings 19:18).

Out of this OT strand of believers, the Messiah came into the world. Through Christ's atoning work and the outpouring of the Spirit at Pentecost, a new people of God emerged. This new people, the church, stands in continuity with the old. For this reason the apostles can carry OT covenant names for God's people over to the church: "chosen race," "royal priesthood," "holy nation," and "God's own people" (1 Pet. 2:9).

Paul even calls the church "the Israel of God" (Gal. 6:16) and "the true circumcision" (Phil. 3:3, GNB). The church is described as "twelve tribes" (James 1:1) and as "exiles of the Dispersion" (1 Pet. 1:1)—the term commonly used for Jews living outside Palestine.

The eternal city is said to have the names of the twelve tribes on its gates, and the names of the twelve apostles on its foundations (Rev. 21:12-14). The twenty-four elders likewise symbolize the patriarchs and the apostles (Rev. 4). These are ways of saying that the entire people of God, comprised of OT and NT saints, will be in the eternal city.

The Dramatic Unity. Let us further illustrate that the Scriptures are a unity but also demonstrate a progressive revelation. We might think of the entire Bible as a divine drama. OT and NT are then two major acts in this drama of redemption. Within these acts of the drama are a great number of scenes.

As we read the Bible, we can understand the words and the impact of the different scenes in the OT. However, to grasp these messages fully, we have to read on. As we come to the NT, the drama takes some interesting turns. Only after the drama is completed can we really understand the significance of earlier scenes. There is continuity in this drama, but there is also discontinuity. God surprises us from time to time by his saving acts.

Someone has compared the history of salvation to a long German sentence: there is a principal clause and many subordinate clauses. We can understand the words in these clauses and what the individual clauses mean. But until the verb is tacked on at the end, we cannot fully understand the sentence. So it is with the Scriptures. We need to grasp that final revelation in Christ. Only then can we better understand all the clauses that preceded it.

If we find apparent contradictions in the long and checkered history of redemption, we should view these like the instructions parents give their children. When a child is small, the parents strictly forbid the child to play with matches. When the child is older, the mother may say, "Please get a match and light the candles." The two commands seem contradictory, but they are not.

Suppose an artist sets out to draw a picture. He begins with a few bold strokes (as, for example, in the OT). He keeps on drawing or painting, adding new strokes, new colors. We begin to guess what the picture will look like, but we may be wrong. Only when the picture is complete can we see what was in the artist's mind. Those first strokes were so different from the final scene, but they still belong to the picture.

Likewise, there are many passages in the OT that we do not immediately understand. But in the light of the complete picture in Christ, we realize that they also belong to the picture. The life, the teachings, the death, and the exaltation of our Lord are essential to our understanding of the Bible as a whole.

Progressive revelation means that God in his grace comes down to us and speaks to us in ways that we can understand. From time to time God tells us more plainly what he has in mind for humanity. Finally, God makes himself known through his Son, Jesus Christ. The Bible is not uniform, but there is a fundamental unity that is not undermined by what we have called progressive revelation.

In the article on Scripture, the *Confession of Faith in a Mennonite Perspective* states succinctly what is meant by progressive revelation:

> We seek to understand and interpret Scripture in harmony with Jesus Christ as we are led by the Holy Spirit in the church. . . . God has spoken above all in the living Word who became flesh and revealed the truth of God faithfully and without deception. (21)

Bibliography

Anchor Bible Dictionary, The (ABD). Ed. D. N. Freedman et al. 6 vols. New York: Doubleday, 1992.

Barclay, W. *Introducing the Bible*. Nashville: Abingdon, 1972, 1997.

Believers Church Bible Commentary Series (BCBC). Scottdale, Pa.: Herald Press, 1986ff.

Berkhof, L. *Principles of Biblical Interpretation*. Grand Rapids: Baker Book House, 1952.

Blackman, E. C. *Biblical Interpretation*. London: Independent, 1957.

Bray, Gerald. *Biblical Interpretation Past and Present*. Downers Grove, Ill.: InterVarsity, 1996.

Bruce, F. F. *The Books and the Parchments: How We Got Our English Bible*. 3d ed. Old Tappan, N.J.: Fleming H. Revell, 1963.

_____. *The Canon of Scripture*. Downers Grove, Ill.: InterVarsity, 1988.

_____. *The History of the Bible in English: From the Earliest Versions to Today*. 3d ed. Oxford: Oxford Univ. Press, 1978.

Caird, G. B. *Language and Imagery of the Bible*. London: Duckworth, 1980; Grand Rapids: Eerdmans, 1997.

Carson, D. A. *Exegetical Fallacies*. Grand Rapids: Baker Book House, 1984, 1996.

Charlesworth, James H., ed. *The Old Testament Pseudepigrapha*. 2 vols. Garden City, N.Y.: Doubleday & Co., 1983-85.

Confession of Faith in a Mennonite Perspective. Scottdale, Pa.: Herald Press, 1995.

Corley, B., S. Lemke, and G. Lovejoy. *Biblical Hermeneutics*. Nashville: Broadman, 1996.

Cullmann, Oscar. *The Early Church*. Philadelphia: Westminster, 1956.

Ewert, David. *From Ancient Tablets to Modern Translations*. Grand Rapids: Zondervan, 1983.

Fee, Gordon D. *The First Epistle to the Corinthians*. The New International Commentary on the New Testament. Grand Rapids: Eerdmans, 1987.

_____ and Douglas Stuart. *How to Read the Bible for All It's Worth*. Grand Rapids: Zondervan, 1982, 1993.

Filson, Floyd V. *Which Books Belong in the Bible?* Philadelphia:
    Westminster, 1957.
Goldingay, John. *Models for Interpretation of Scripture.* Grand Rapids:
    Eerdmans, 1995.
_____. *Models for Scripture.* Grand Rapids: Eerdmans, 1994.
Grant, Robert M. *A Short History of the Interpretation of the Bible.*
    New York: Macmillan, 1972; with David Tracy, rev. ed.,
    Philadelphia: Fortress, 1984.
Green, Joel. *Hearing the New Testament.* Grand Rapids: Eerdmans,
    1995.
HarperCollins Bible Dictionary (HCBD). Ed. Paul J. Achtemeier with
    Society of Biblical Literature. Rev. ed. San Francisco:
    Harper San Francisco, 1996.
Harrington, Daniel J. *Interpreting the New Testament.* Wilmington:
    Michael Glazier, 1979; Collegeville, Minn.: Liturgical, 1990.
Hunter, A. M. *Probing the New Testament.* Richmond: John Knox,
    1971.
Job, John B., ed. *How to Study the Bible.* Downers Grove, Ill.:
    InterVarsity, 1972.
Klein, W. W., C. L. Blomberg, and R. L. Hubbard. *Introduction to
    Biblical Interpretation.* Dallas: Word, 1993.
Lind, Millard C. *Yahweh Is a Warrier: The Theology of Warfare in
    Ancient Israel.* Scottdale, Pa.: Herald Press, 1980.
Longenecker, Richard. *Biblical Exegesis in the Apostolic Period.* Grand
    Rapids: Eerdmans, 1975; 2d ed., 1999.
Marshall, I. Howard. *New Testament Interpretation: Essays on
    Principles and Methods.* Grand Rapids: Eerdmans, 1966.
Metzger, Bruce M. *The Canon of the New Testament.* Oxford: Oxford
    Univ. Press, 1987; reprint ed., 1997.
_____. *Introduction to the Apocrypha.* Oxford: Oxford Univ. Press,
    1957, 1977.
_____. *The Text of the New Testament.* 3d ed. Oxford: Oxford Univ.
    Press, 1992.
Michelson, A. Berkeley. *Interpreting the Bible.* Grand Rapids:
    Eerdmans, 1963.
Michelson, A. Berkeley, and Alvera Michelson. *Understanding
    Scripture.* Ventura, Calif.: Regal Books, 1982.
Morris, Leon. *I Believe in Revelation.* Grand Rapids: Eerdmans, 1976.
Neill, Stephen. *The Interpretation of the New Testament 1861-1961.*
    Oxford: Oxford Univ. Press, 1964. 2d ed.: *The Interpretation
    of the New Testament 1861-1986.* 1988.
Ramm, Bernhard L. *Protestant Biblical Hermeneutics.* Grand Rapids:
    Baker Book House, 1967. 3d ed.: *Protestant Biblical
    Interpretation: A Textbook of Hermeneutics.* 1980.
Roop, Eugene F. *Genesis.* BCBC. Scottdale, Pa.: Herald Press, 1987.

Silva, Moises. *Biblical Words and Their Meaning.* Grand Rapids: Zondervan, 1983.

_____. *Has the Church Misread the Bible? The History of Interpretation in the Light of Contemporary Issues.* Grand Rapids: Zondervan, 1987.

Schroeder, David. *Learning to Know the Bible.* Scottdale, Pa.: Herald Press, 1966.

Smart, James. *The Interpretation of Scripture.* Philadelphia: Westminster, 1961.

_____. *The Strange Silence of the Bible in the Church.* Philadelphia: Westminster, 1970.

Sproul, R. C. *Knowing Scripture.* Downers Grove, Ill.: InterVarsity, 1977.

Stein, Robert. *Playing by the Rules.* Grand Rapids: Baker Book House, 1994.

Sterrett, T. Norton. *How to Understand the Bible.* Downers Grove, Ill.: InterVarsity, 1974. Ed. with John Job: *How to Understand Your Bible.* 1982.

Stewart, James S. *The Gates of New Life.* New York: Scribner.

Stibbs, Alan. M. *Understanding God's Word.* London: Inter-Varsity, 1961.

_____, ed. *Search the Scriptures.* Downers Grove, Ill.: InterVarsity, 1984.

Stott, John R. W. *Understanding the Bible.* Glendale: Regal Books, 1972. Rev. ed: Grand Rapids: Zondervan, 1999.

Swartley, Willard M. *Slavery, Sabbath, War, and Women.* Scottdale, Pa.: Herald Press, 1983.

_____, ed. *Essays on Biblical Interpretation: Anabaptist-Mennonite Perspectives.* Elkhart, Ind.: Institute of Mennonite Studies, 1984.

Thistleton, A. C. *The Two Horizons.* Grand Rapids: Eerdmans, 1980.

Waltner, Erland, and J. Daryl Charles. *1-2 Peter, Jude.* BCBC. Scottdale, Pa.: Herald Press, 1999.

Wenger, J. C. *God's Word Written.* Scottdale, Pa.: Herald Press, 1966.

Yoder, Perry B. *Toward Understanding the Bible.* Newton, Kan.: Faith & Life Press, 1978.

Scripture Index

The Author

David Ewert was born in Russia of German-speaking parents. The family emigrated in the 1920s and eventually settled on a farm in western Canada. There David received his elementary education, followed by five years of biblical studies at several Bible schools.

Ewert earned degrees from the University of British Columbia (B.A.); Central Baptist Seminary, Toronto (B.D.); Wheaton College (M.A.); Luther Seminary, St. Paul (M.Th.); and McGill University, Montreal (Ph.D.).

The Mennonite Brethren Biblical Seminary, Fresno, California, recently awarded him an honorary Doctor of Divinity degree.

After teaching in Bible schools for seven years, Ewert taught Greek and biblical exegesis at the Mennonite Brethren Bible College (later Concord College, and now Canadian Mennonite University), Winnipeg, for twenty-five years. He also served as president of MBBC. For several years, he also taught Greek and New Testament at Mennonite Brethren Biblical Seminary and at Eastern Mennonite Seminary, Harrisonburg, Virginia.

Ewert has been visiting professor at various seminaries in India, Africa, Latin America, and Europe, as well as at a number of colleges and seminaries in North America. Even while generally retired, he continues to teach courses each year in Bonn, Germany. Because of his German-speaking ability, he has been on numerous preaching missions in Switzerland, Austria, and Germany. He still speaks at Bible conferences and ministers retreats in Canada and abroad.

The author has published more than a dozen books in English and several in German. He has written several volumes in the Luminaire Series of biblical interpretation for Kindred Press. He has also provided many chapters for other books and contributed widely to periodicals.

Ewert has written articles for reference works such as *Harper's Bible Dictionary*, *The Mennonite Encyclopedia*, *Dictionary of Christianity in America*, and *The Oxford Companion to the Bible*. His autobiography, *A Journey of Faith*, was published by Kindred Press in 1993.

David Ewert is married to Lena Hamm. They have five grown children (four daughters and one son) and twelve grandchildren. The Ewerts are members of the Bakerview Mennonite Brethren Church, Abbotsford, British Columbia.